MAORI
GAMES & HAKA

INSTRUCTIONS, WORDS & ACTIONS

ALAN ARMSTRONG

ILLUSTRATED BY BARRY ELLIS AND L. C. MITCHELL

REED

Reed Publishing (NZ) Ltd
Te Karuhi tā tāpui o Reed (Aotearoa)

Established in 1907, Reed is New Zealand's largest
book publisher, with over 300 titles in print.

For details on all these books visit our website:
www.reed.co.nz

Published by Reed Books, a division of Reed Publishing (NZ) Ltd, 39 Rawene Road, Birkenhead, Auckland 10. Associated companies, branches and representatives throughout the world.

© 2005 The Estate of Alan G. Armstrong
The author asserts his moral rights in the work.

ISBN 0 7900 1016 X
This edition first published 2005

First edition published 1964 by A.H. & A.W. Reed Ltd
Reprinted 1974

National Library of New Zealand Cataloguing-in-Publication Data

Armstrong, Alan, 1933-1986.
Māori games & haka : instructions, words and actions / Alan G. Armstrong ; illustrated by Barry Ellis and L.C. Mitchell. New ed.
Originally published as: Maori games and hakas. 1964.
ISBN 0-7900-1016-X
1. Maori (New Zealand people)—Games. 2. Maori (New Zealand people)—Recreation. 3. Haka (Dance) 4. Folk dancing, Maori.
I. Armstrong, Alan, 1933-1986. Maori games and hakas. II. Ellis, Barry. III. Mitchell, L. C. IV. Title.
790.08999442—dc 22

Text illustrations by Barry Ellis and L.C. Mitchell
Front cover: Maori warriors performing a haka.
Front cover photo: Tim Graham/Alamy
Cover design by Cathy Bignell
Printed in New Zealand

ACKNOWLEDGMENTS

Errors, omissions and inadequacies in this book are solely my responsibility. Throughout its preparation, however, I have been helped by many friends, Maori and Pakeha, whose names are too numerous, unfortunately, to list here. They include valued friends in the Ngati Poneke Young Maori Club and the Concert Party of the 2nd Battalion the New Zealand Regiment. They variously posed for the photographs on which the illustrations are based, offered advice, criticism and information and sustained me with interest and encouragement.

I acknowledge with gratitude the permission granted by Mr D. Alexander of Rotorua to consult and make use of his notes on hand games collected while teaching among Tuhoe (See Part Two, Maori Games).

In particular, however, I must single out for mention those who were kind enough to teach me material previously unknown to me, and others who patiently read through and criticised the completed manuscript. They are:

Kingi Ihaka	Reupena Ngata
Hoani (John) Waititi	Tarutaru Rankin
George Reedy	Arapeta Awatere
Brownie Puriri	Beth Ranapia

To all these people I would like to say: Kei te mihi atu au ki nga hoa maha mo nga manaakitanga me nga awhina e taea te kore e korero engari ka mau tonu i roto i te ngakau. Tena koutou katoa.

CONTENTS

FOREWORD

I leave you to dream the dream
That I and many friends have treasured
throughout the years.
That worthwhile elements of the old Maori
culture,
the things that belong to this beautiful land,
may be preserved for the New Zealand Nation.

Sir Apirana Ngata.

To the Maori people their rich cultural heritage will always remain a strong source of spiritual satisfaction and a vigorous expression of their pride of race. However, as well as being symbolic of a mighty past, it is also one of the means to a hopeful future.

This book has been written both as a manual of instruction and as a minor work of reference. As a manual of instruction it may be of assistance to those people — Maori and Pakeha — who wish to participate actively in Maori cultural activities.

I hope that Pakeha in particular will find it a useful stepping stone towards joining with the Maori in those group activities which are so much a part of their Maoritanga — their pride of race. I feel that in the realm of shared cultural activities, there lies one of the important meeting places for our two races.

Secondly, as a work of reference this book aims to give those who are interested the means to study in some detail the mechanics of those aspects of ancient and modern Maori culture which are most real and commonplace to the average Maori today. It is hoped that these and other facets of Maori culture will gradually become woven into the fabric of a common national culture, appreciated by, and felt to belong to, all New Zealanders, irrespective of race.

Alan Armstrong.
Wellington, May 1964

PREFACE

It is important that at the beginning of the book, the non-Maori reader should understand the importance to the Maori people of those things with which the book deals, namely, Maori songs, games and dances, and appreciate why, in this modern day and age, these things should be considered worth preserving and writing about.

In time the culture of the numerically dominant Pakeha race gradually imposed itself on the pattern of Maori life. This process produced many stresses and strains which left their mark on the emerging racial partnership.

Now, one hundred and fifty years later, New Zealanders are, by and large, one people. Maori live, work and play in the same manner as all other citizens of this country. Almost every facet of their daily life is bound up in extricably with that of the Pakeha. For most young Maori, English is their first language and many know no other.

Being a Maori in New Zealand today is not so much a question of skin colour as having a certain state of mind. One of the most important attributes of being a Maori is awareness of, and a fierce pride in, certain aspects of traditional Maori culture. Principally these are the Maori language, Maori ceremonial and protocol (te kawa o te marae), Maori history and legend and Maori songs, dances and games.

I believe that the order in which I have placed these aspects of Maori culture is the order of their importance. Unfortunately, however, by virtue of environment and opportunity, many Maori have, at best, a very limited knowledge of their own language. Similarly, to many who live in the city or in 'detribalised' rural communities, marae ceremonial and protocol is unknown except perhaps in some of its most elementary observances. Therefore, to a very large number of Maori, the most real and immediate manifestation of their culture and the most tangible expression, of racial identity are their songs, games and dances. Theses are the things which even in a city they can grow up with and learn from the cradle without conscious effort. In cities particularly, when Maori come together they might speak English, but the gathering will be different from that of Pakeha because sooner or later those present will express their moods and emotions in a distinctively Maori way — by songs and haka.

Many Pakeha New Zealanders also have an interest in these things for two reasons. First because they are intrinsically artistic and beautiful; and secondly because a knowledge of Maori songs and dances, and an ability to perform them, gives the Pakeha an entré into Maori social life, and a community of interest and friendship with the Maori people which is richly rewarding and warmly satisfying.

Scope

This book concerns itself only with the games and dances (and indirectly songs) of the Maori people which are traditional in origin and which are still current today. Background and historical material has also been included for without it the main theme loses much of its interest and meaning. The book is divided into four parts.

Part 1 is a miscellany — the language (a very brief survey), teaching technique (for I hope that teachers will have a use for this book) and sparring movements with the spearlike taiaha. This latter is a dying art. It was taught to me years ago by my old friend, Hone Heke Rankin, chieftain of Nga Puhi, and this is a convenient place in which to give it permanent record. Concert entrances, a facet of Maori performance often sadly neglected, are also included.

Part 2 deals with Maori games. Many of the ancient games are no longer played. These have been dealt with in an introductory chapter. Three traditional games, however, are still common and these have merited chapters of their own and have been illustrated in some detail so that they can be easily learned.

Part 3 deals with the musical dances — that is, those dances performed to a musical rhythm — and includes powhiri (dance of welcome), action song and poi (long and short). Again the treatment is instructional. Historical and background data are followed by notes on performance technique and by examples. Each example has Maori words with translation, music where applicable, and then the actions illustrated with explanatory notes so that they can be learned by the novice.

Finally comes Part 4, which for the most part breaks completely new ground. The subject is the shouted posture dance, commonly (but not strictly accurately) termed haka. The same treatment has been followed as with the other dances, except that instead of music the words are broken down to show the rhythm in which they are intoned.

Many Maori words are used throughout the text, and a glossary has been included at the end of the book.

Each part is prefaced by an introduction which details the scope and treatment of what is to follow. This should be read first. The historical and background material is also essential reading if the subject is to be fully understood.

The publishers claim, with some justifications, that this is the most complex book which they have ever produced, and I am grateful indeed for the infinite pains which they have taken in its production.

PART ONE

INTRODUCTION

1

THE MAORI LANGUAGE

Introduction. As one of the aims of this book is to introduce the uninitiated to Maori culture, the starting point must obviously be at least a superficial knowledge of the Maori language and an ability to pronounce it with something approaching correctness.

The Nature of the Language. The Maori language is phonetic, that is, it is pronounced to all intents and purposes as it is spelt. There are fifteen letters. The vowels are a, e, i, o, u, and the consonants are h, k, m, n, ng, p, t, w, wh. 'Ng' and 'wh' have been classed as letters because they form single sounds which are not exactly represented in the English language.

Maori is a dialect of the language spoken throughout Polynesia. As such it has an affinity with most languages spoken in the Pacific and Southeast Asia.

For example:

Within the language itself there are differences between tribes and districts but these are lessening with the passage of time and do not prevent Maori throughout New Zealand from understanding one another.

Tribal Differences in Spoken Maori. Between various tribes there are differences in emphasis and intonation. In some areas Maori speak in a sing-song manner and in others they speak more quickly and in a more staccato fashion. The 'wh' sound is variously rendered as 'wh', 'h', 'hw' and 'f'. Amongst the Tuhoe people of the Bay of Plenty and in parts of the South Island the 'ng' becomes a straight 'n' while the Ngai Tahu tribe substitute 'k' for 'ng' in many words.

There are some minor differences in vocabulary and some tribes are more addicted than others to transliterate forms and the interjection of English words and phrases. As an example of a minor

	Maori	*Fiji*	*Samoa*	*Solomon Is.*	*Malaya*	*Tahiti*	*Caroline Is.*
Sky	rangi	lagi	lagi	dangi	langit	ra,i	rangi
Stone	whatu	vatu	fatu	vatu	batu	fatu	patu
Eye	mata	mata	mata	mata	mata	mata	mata
Five	rima	lima	lima	lima	lima	rima	elima

vocabulary variation, we have the common Maori term of address 'e hoa' (oh friend). However 'e kare' is the equivalent among the people of the Waikato and on the East Coast 'e hika' is a frequently used mode of address. Two other terms of address used in certain areas are 'e mara' for both sexes and 'e kara' for older men only.

Pronunciation of Maori. Given below are greatly simplified rules for the pronunciation of Maori. Each vowel has a short and long sound and these can alter the meaning of the word. No attempt is made in this book to show which are the long and which are short sounds.

Vowels: The *approximate* sounds are:

a — as in m*a*rk (long a) or as in c*u*t (short a)

e — as in a sound in between b*e*t and w*eigh*t (long e) or as in b*e*t (short e)

i — as in f*ee*d (long i) or as in f*i*t (short i)

o — as in f*o*rk (long o) or as in vi*o*let (short o)

u — as in sp*oo*n (long u) or as in s*oo*t (short u)

Maori vowel sounds are very much more pure and rounded than the English equivalent.

Consonants: These are pronounced much the same as in English. Note the following:

r — The r is not rolled.

ng — This is a nasalised sound as in si*ng*ing. It must not be pronounced as a straight n sound or as the ng in finger.

wh —While some parts, especially the far North, still give wh its pre-European sound of an aspirated w (hw as in *wh*en) the pronunciation of wh as 'f' is now definitely the more common.

Syllables. A beginner attempting to pronounce Maori should divide difficult words into syllables and pronounce each syllable slowly at first and then more quickly until the whole word flows smoothly. A syllable in Maori is either a vowel on its own or a consonant followed by a vowel ('wh' and 'ng' count as single consonants). Examples:

Ngaruawahia — Nga / ru / a / wa / hi / a,

Whangarei — Wha / nga / re / i.

Emphasis. Maori words are generally emphasised slightly on the first syllable, e.g. *ta*ngata. Some compound words are given a greater degree of emphasis on the second portion of the word, e.g. *wha*kah*o*ki.

2

TEACHING HAKA AND ACTION SONGS

Technique. Technique is important when teaching both haka taparahi and action song. Often they are taught very badly if the end result is any criterion. Some of this is caused by group leaders trying to get their charges to run before they can walk and by leaving faults to iron themselves out instead of constantly checking and correcting and never being satisfied by anything less than the very best.

All leaders have their own style of teaching and it would be presumptuous to lay down hard and fast rules. However, attention to the points mentioned below will usually result in more polished performances, more confident performers and a much better result achieved in less time. At the end are some points for those teaching themselves.

Explaining the Item. It is very important that performers understand the nature and significance of the items. This is too often neglected. The result is an unconvincing performance and vague actions because the performers do not understand just what they are trying to say. Leaders often forget that sometimes even quite competent users of colloquial Maori cannot translate, without help, the literary style found in some taparahi and waiata where archaic words and usage serve to obscure the meaning for present-day speakers of the language. Taparahi and action songs all express a message. Obviously this will be completely lacking in sincerity if it is not understood. Therefore a translation, or at least a general explanation, of the item must always be given when introducing it to a group for the first time.

The Words. One haka teacher of my acquaintance always begins his teaching sessions with practice of the vowel sounds. This is to be recommended even with experienced groups and is especially important with those containing a high proportion of young people. Maori speech today has become so corrupted by the flat, tight-lipped English vowel sounds that this preliminary is valuable for vocal limbering-up and does not by any means represent wasted time.

The next step is to learn the words (and tune in the case of an action song) thoroughly before any actions are attempted. There is often a great temptation to get onto the actions quickly and the result is either mumbled, indistinct words because everyone is too busy watching the leader to follow the words, or poor actions because performers have their eyes glued to a blackboard. Merely running through the words time after time is not sufficient. Difficult lines must be broken down and the beats and breath pauses explained. Leaders must listen carefully and note slurring and faltering which marks uncertainty with words. Unless such faults are corrected early they are difficult to eradicate and can persist for a long time.

The words may be left up before the performers when they begin the actions but should be removed after a time so that they must learn the words off by heart. In final stages of rehearsal, leaders should watch very carefully. Performers who still don't know the words correctly should be given extra help, and finally, if their services are not dispensed with, relegated to the back row. As with all teams, there is little room for idle passengers, especially in a good tapahari group, but if a performer is obviously trying hard then he should be encouraged in every way. If time and circumstances permit, a little private tuition may help.

Actions. Many of the remarks above apply similarly to learning the actions, particularly the reference to the value of private tuition. Just as it is a good idea to practise sounds, so it is often helpful — particularly when there are a number of inexperienced members in the group — to carry out practice exercises before getting on to the actual actions. This allows everyone to limber up, gives novices confidence and allows the group leader to move around correcting common faults in posture and execution. The basis for a set of exercises is given at the end of the chapter.

Too often the actions are just repeated time after time. Initially the action song or taparahi may lend itself to being broken down line by line or into groups of lines, the actions of each being taken through slowly with the performers following. Difficult actions must be fully demonstrated and the performers given a few minutes to practise in their own time, those in difficulty being corrected by more experienced members of the group.

Opinions differ as to whether the items should be practised in correct tempo right from the beginning. I personally favour taking items with difficult words and or actions through slowly at first, but I must readily admit that this often has the disadvantage of making the beat more difficult to establish and causing people to progressively slow down to the original practice tempo even after the correct speed is finally established and practised. Once pronunciation and phrasing are mastered, the words must be taken through at their correct speed. In other words, as the words are learned so must also the rhythm be learned. To get this rhythm, beating time with the foot is the best method. This is one of the essential parts of preliminary learning.

Correcting Faults. The important thing is that faults are straightened out as the rehearsal progresses. Nevertheless it is best not to correct individuals while the rest of the group waits. This will cause novices in particular to lose confidence. Specific faults in individuals are best brought to notice by a general reference to them. This generalised correction should, however, be supplemented if possible by experienced performers moving around among the group during the course of the item correcting individual errors, and helping those in difficulty.

Formation. Novices are usually understandably reluctant to get into the front and tend to hide away at the back where they can neither see nor be seen and their faults corrected. Spread the performers out and allow plenty of space between rows and individuals. Sprinkle experienced performers among the inexperienced.

The Leader. He is the conductor of our orchestra, yet often he cannot be seen by the musicians. During rehearsals he should stand on a table or similar platform with his back to the performers. The disadvantage of course is that his actions are partially obscured, but many performers find it difficult to follow when the leader is facing them and making his actions in opposite directions to theirs. If the leader does lead with his back to the group then it will first be necessary for a careful demonstration of actions while facing the group. The idea is to have two leaders — one facing and the other turned away from the group.

In later rehearsals, it is a good idea to dispense with a leader in front altogether. Some performers seem to become mesmerised by the leader and keep their eyes glued on him throughout. In the action song the eyes must follow the hand movement. In the taparahi the eyes generally watch the audience.

Summary. In summary therefore, a suggested sequence of teaching is:
1   Introduce the item. Say what it is, taparahi, peruperu etc. and if necessary explain what a taparahi is. Mention the history of the item if

known and then give a translation, either line by line or in general terms.

2 Practise the vowel sounds. Select some difficult words from the piece and get the group to pronounce them.

3 Practise the words without actions until a good standard is reached. Use the opportunity to practise rhythm as well, by beating time with the foot.

4 Run the group through practice exercises.

5 Get some of the experienced performers who already know the item (if any are available) to run through the words and actions completely at the correct speed.

6 Practise the actions, slowly at first and line by line.

7 Remove the words from before the performers, practise at correct speed and finally perform the item with the leader in rear instead of in front.

Again I emphasise that this is a suggested sequence. Depending on the experience of the group, and the number who know the item initially, some of these steps can be omitted. There are, however no grounds for omitting the steps purely because of the time factor as I am convinced that attention to these points will usually produce a more polished result in a shorter time.

Teaching Yourself. The best and quickest way to learn is to join a Maori cultural group. These groups often welcome newcomers, including Pakeha, and will go out of their way to overcome initial shyness.

If however, no course is available, then you will have to start to teach yourself from a book. In such circumstances, you will find the action song much easier to learn than the haka taparahi. The first step is to learn to read and pronounce Maori, or at least to sing it, with reasonable facility. The important thing when teaching yourself is not to attempt too much at once. Dispose of the words first of all and then you can give your wholehearted attention to learning the actions.

The next step is to master the practice actions,

first to counting and then at action song tempo. Once confidence has been gained in this way, comes the more difficult task of marrying up words, tune and actions. *Me He Manu Rere* is recommended as a straightforward song. *Poutini* is a suitably simple haka. If possible, always practise in front of a mirror. Even experienced exponents should not scorn this when learning a new item on their own. Finally, if it is possible, get a friend to criticise.

SOME PRACTICE EXERCISES

Style. These exercises can be used for both action song and taparahi. The styles of actions for these two dances of course differ greatly and the practice exercises will help performers to adjust themselves to the appropriate style before commencing an actual item. In the action song, the emphasis is on gracefulness. The actions flow rhythmically, one into the other. The movements are fluid yet controlled. Many male performers do not seem to realise this and fling their bodies around in an abandonment which should be reserved for the haka taparahi. In this the emphasis is on masculinity. The actions are vigorous and exaggerated. Latent power is expressed at all times, exploding into a violent outburst of energy at the climax of the dance. Too often with younger performers the less forceful actions of the action song are carried over into the taparahi.

Group Use of the Exercises. The leader will begin by calling 'Waewae takahia' and the group practises the foot movement. This can continue for as long as is thought necessary, in time to counting or, in the case of action song to music. Then the leader may call 'Ringa e whiua' (swing the hands) and the second exercise is begun. This is followed by the remaining exercises with the leader designating the exercise by its number or some other method.

1 — THE ACTION OF THE FEET

Action Song

 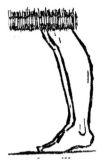

There are two common styles illustrated above. On the left the right foot beats time, merely leaving the ground a few inches. In action songs in waltz time, however, the movement is more exaggerated with the right foot swinging off the ground for some 150 mm up behind the left leg. On the right, the feet do not leave the ground at all. The beat is marked by a raising and lowering of the body from the ball of the foot, the heel leaving the ground a few inches (This latter is used only by some tribes.) Get the performers to practise the beat with their hands on the hips.

Haka Taparahi

The taparahi foot movement is basically the action song foot movement but with more emphasis. The right foot may clear the ground by up to a foot and the left knee is bent. As will be seen the feet are well apart and the back must not be bent.

Peruperu

(a) (b)

(c) (d)

For some movements the foot action will be as for the haka taparahi. In others it will be as illustrated above. To begin, the feet are about 300 mm apart at the heel with the body weight evenly on the centre line (a). With a hop the left foot comes into the centre while the right leg swings up so that the heel almost touches the buttocks (b). As the right leg comes to the ground again, the left foot resumes its former position (a).

Another peruperu foot action is illustrated in (c). It is a leap off the ground with both feet together. As the body is off the ground the feet kick up behind to try and touch the buttocks. It is important with this movement that the kick comes from the knees and there is NO bending at the waist. The upper leg remains straight.

The action shown in (d) is simply a leaping off the ground from side to side.

In some Arawa peruperu there is a foot movement in which the right foot is carried off to the left so that the whole body turns left. It is graceful and intricate and cannot be suitably illustrated.

Another variant I have seen only among Tuhoe but may also be used by other tribes. It is often (but not exclusively) used when taparahi are performed inside a meeting house. Basically it is the movement (at bottom left of page 17) except that instead of the whole right foot coming off the ground, only the heel or toes are raised. The left leg is not raised at all.

2 — HAND SWING

For this exercise the hands are in front of the body, forearms parallel to the ground, palms facing in.

The hands move across the body in time to the beat. This movement is basically the same in both haka and action song except that in the haka the hands move a greater distance across the body. This exercise is useful to ensure that the performers are 'wiri-ing' correctly. Wiri is the trembling movement of the hands and forearm which shows a person is really 'with it' when he is doing action songs or haka. Inexperienced performers use an ugly wriggling of the fingers in the belief that they are doing the correct 'wiri' but the tremble emanates from the elbow and affects the whole forearm, wrist and hand.

3 — THE HAERE MAI ACTION

This is an action song action. Get the group to move from the left hand action to the right changing position on each musical beat. It is a useful exercise as it practises interchange from one action to another in time to a beat. Ensure the change is smooth and flowing.

Head Movement. The head and eyes should follow the upraised hand: it is a combination of four different things — head movement, wiri, the action itself, and movement from one action to another — and thus practises co-ordination.

4 — THE TORONA KI WAHO MOVEMENT

In the action song, the hands are extended gracefully and then the chest is lightly patted.

In the haka the hands are thrust forward, with the right foot going forward about 150 mm and the body weight taken on a bent left leg. The body straightens up as the hands are brought in and the chest slap should leave a red mark on the flesh.

5 — THE KNEE SLAP

The difference between the action song and haka action is merely one of degree. The important thing with this exercise is that it will serve to correct the common fault of sagging or leaning forward at the waist. The hands reach the thighs by bending the knees and carrying the right foot slightly forward. The trunk remains upright and the eyes look forward.

6 — THE ELBOW SLAP

This is a good taparahi exercise. It involves a change between two postures. In the first action the position is crouching. This crouch must come from the legs and not by a leaning forward from the waist. The body straightens up on the second action. The slap of hand on flesh should resound and leave red marks on the flesh.

3

A DRILL FOR THE TAIAHA

The Weapon

In the days gone by, the taiaha or hani was one of the principal weapons of the Maori fighting man. Used by the skilful warrior in battle, it was a weapon to be reckoned with, and an old proverb warns of the tongue of a woman in peace and the tongue of a taiaha in war!

The taiaha was a sophisticated development of the pouwhenua, which although much more effective as a weapon, was less highly regarded a a chiefly staff than the more elaborately carved and decorated taiaha. Taiaha were made of a strong, dense-grained hardwood such as manuka. Such woods gave strength combined with lightness. A good taiaha would weigh little more than 500g. Dimensions varied according to the needs of the user. Generally they were 150-180cm long.

One end, known as the arero, was usually elaborately carved and shaped like a human tongue. This proximal end could be used for stabbing. Between tongue and shaft was a carved, styled representation of the human head which could be decorated with eyes of paua or similar shell. Taiaha kura had a band of bright red feathers fastened to a woven strip of material called taui kura. This went around the shaft just below the head. Tufts of white dog hair were sometimes also fixed to protrude below the feathers.

Arero (Weapons are illustrated in full on page 127).

The shaft ran down gradually, widening and flattening until the blade was some 75mm wide and 5-10mm thick.

Contrary to popular belief, the taiaha is not a spear but a long handled club. It was not thrown, but used somewhat in the manner of the old English quarterstaff. With the blade uppermost, the warrior would parry the strokes of his enemy until the moment came for a blow to the head or body, or the quick turning-off of the enemy's weapon, while the tongue of the taiaha came up and pierced the unguarded stomach. Today as is only to be expected, the wielding of the taiaha is a dying art. It still has its place during the ceremonial challenge on the marae, and in the peruperu, but as a fighting weapon it is seen no more.

The Drill

Set out below is a simple exercise with the taiaha which incorporates some of the ancient techniques of handling this weapon. After a little practice the drill can make a really spectacular concert item. It consists of five attack positions and five guard or defence positions. Each of these guard positions is a perfect counter to one of the attack positions. Thus two performers go rapidly through the drill, one employing the attack positions from one to five, while the other counters him, using the equivalent defensive positions. When the set of five is complete, the warrior who has been defending goes over to the attack while his opponent assumes the defence. This change-over between players can be repeated for any desired number of times. Finally, after the battle has raged back and forth, the defender goes to his knees in the fifth position. Quickly the other brings his taiaha up to his opponent's stomach and with a realistic death cry the battle is ended. To the audience, the crack as taiaha meets taiaha, the quick footwork of the warriors and their lightning changes of position, coupled with fierce war whoops and pukana, make a thrilling enactment of an age-old battle drill.

The Approach

In advancing into battle with the taiaha, or on the stage for the enactment of the drill, the taiaha is held in the position known as marangai areare.

As shown in the illustration, the club is horizontal and level with the shoulders, the blade lying along the back of the neck and the tongue pointing out to the right. This is an attitude of defiance, and the warrior's breast is exposed in contemptuous challenge. Both arms should be outstretched and the advance is made with short, mincing steps. The warrior inclines his body alternately from side to side, fiercely grimacing and making little shrill, yelping cries. From this position a player will sometimes assume the hoi position, allowing the blade to swing out behind the body, pointing rearwards and the tongue of the weapon resting against the hoi or earlobe.

Tradition has it that if the warrior and weapon are in perfect concord a message is transmitted to the taiaha telling it what to do.

Once the opponents come within striking distance they assume the normal guard position, poupoutahi, so that the taiaha covers the front of the body with the blade pointing up.

In this stance the weapon is best placed to parry any attacking blows as well as to take the opportunity to exploit any mistakes by the enemy and deliver a mortal blow from above (whitiapu) with the blade or a thrust from below (whakarehu) with the tongue. There are other guard positions, including one huanui, for use against a left hander, but poupoutahi is generally conceded to cover the body best.

Experienced wielders of the taiaha seldom watched an opponent's weapon, but instead kept their eyes fixed on vital muscles which were a tell-tale indication as to whether a blow was merely a feint or the real thing. The shoulder muscles served this purpose, as did the toes. A feint came from the elbows and did not require a firm stance. A real thrust required the strength of the shoulders and a firm stance, which was indicated by the flexing of the toes as they took up their grip on the earth.

THE POSITIONS

First position

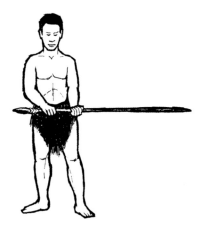

Attacking

From the guard position (poupoutahi) shown previously, the taiaha is brought down until it is horizontal for a forward stroke. The left hand grips under the shaft ,the right hand grips over.

Defending

As the attacking stroke is directed towards the defender's unprotected right side, he must bring his taiaha over from poupoutahi to guard the right side. He does this simply by crossing his arms. There is no change in grip from that used with poupoutahi.

Second position

Attacking

For the second attacking stroke, the taiaha is merely brought back to the poupoutahi guard position and a forward stroke made from there.

Defending

To counter this, the taiaha is brought to a vertical position from the previous defensive position, and the right shoulder is thus protected. There is no change in grip.

Third Position

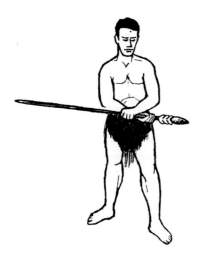

Attacking

Now the other side of the opponent's body is attacked. The grip on the weapon is not changed, but by crossing the arms the attacker achieves a horizontal stroke to the left side of his opponent.

Defending

The defender must speedily bring his taiaha down from the vertical to protect his left side from the waist down.

Fourth Position

Attacking

From the previous position the attacker brings his taiaha up to make a stroke from the right shoulder.

Defending

To counter this stroke, the defender protects his left shoulder by bringing the taiaha vertically up to cover the shoulder.

Fifth Position

Attacking

The taiaha is brought up into a vertical position and a downward stroke made at the opponent's head.

Defending

To protect the head the taiaha is brought up above the head to take the force of the downward stroke. Notice there is no alteration of the hand grip but the left hand slides down the shaft nearer the blade.

The Complete Drill

Now we illustrate the complete drill with the above positions combined. It will be noticed that in each of the above illustrations the performers had a different leg to the fore. This is because in the actual drill there is continual movement: the attacker pressing forward and the defender retreating, even if only slightly, then as the roles are reversed (see below) after the fifth position, the direction of movement changes. As in the sketches above, the two performers may be distinguished by their dress. The attacker is wearing a maro — a small triangular loin cloth, usually covering only the front, worn by warriors — and the defender is clad in a rapaki — a kilt-like garment made from flax and decorated with flaxen thrums and reaching to just above the knees. Often, however, warriors fought without any clothing and at other times they simply wore a belt.

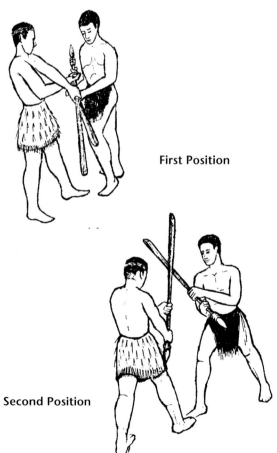

First Position

Second Position

24

Third Position

Fourth Position

Fifth Position

Reversing the Roles

After the five positions have been completed, as illustrated above, the roles change and the defender takes the initiative and goes into the attacking positions, while his opponent is forced into the defensive.

illustration) by whipping in for a horizontal stroke to his opponent's right side. This is, of course, the first attacking position, and the erstwhile attacker must now protect himself by bringing his taiaha rapidly across to the first defensive position.

The defender (on the left in the illustration above) now lunges forward and uses his horizontal taiaha to force the erstwhile attacker back until the latter is forced to step backwards to retain his balance. Immediately this happens the performer presses home his advantage (bottom right hand

So the drill continues until finally, after the battle has raged back and forth, the attacker is forced back to his knees from the fifth position, and quickly his opponent steps in either with a butt stroke to the head or the tongue rips up the unprotected belly or chest. The curtain closes!

4

CONCERT ENTRANCES

If groups are performing on a properly outfitted stage with a curtain, the problem of getting neatly before the audience is simple. However, many performances take place on the marae, on curtainless stages or in other improvised surroundings. The polish of a performance is irretrievably spoiled right from the beginning if the group merely straggles untidily onto the stage or platform. Most groups therefore improvise some sort of a concert entrance which will bring performers from the sidelines into their area of presentation. Several examples of such entrances are given below. They should not be copied but are merely presented for study and comparison. Usually groups will devise their own signature tune for use as an entrance and actions to go with it.

There is considerable controversy as to the side of the stage or marae from which performers enter, and even whether, from the viewpoint of historical precedent, women should be permitted to precede the men. The traditional tama-tane approach, with the men in front of the women prescribes that the entrance be from the LEFT of the stage (that is, from the audience's RIGHT). This ensures that the left arm (the 'ringa whakapuru'

or shield arm) is towards the enemy (in this case, the audience) ready to parry a blow if attacked, while the 'ringa patu' or weapon arm is held back, protected and ready to strike if necessary. This tama-tane approach from the LEFT was one of the early conventions adopted for the action song, particularly among the Ngati Porou.

On the other hand, however, tama-wahine—the approach from RIGHT with the women in front — has equally sound historical precedent among some tribes. In such tribes there was a set protocol on occasions when two groups met for the purpose of making peace. It was customary for the visiting party to assemble on the marae first. The local warriors would then enter from the opposite side in column. They were led by a single file of the picked female dancers of the tribe in their best clothes. Once in front of the visitors, the women would halt and face them, while the men of the home group fell in behind them. Once all was quiet, the women dancers turned sharply left on a signal from their leader and in single file with slow steps in time to a chanted song walked slowly around the left flank of their own men. As she walked, each girl waved her left arm as if beckoning the late enemies

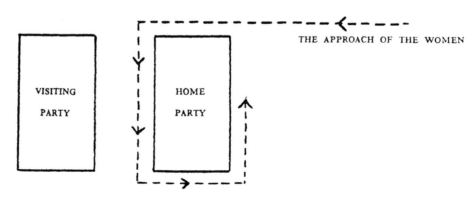

THE APPROACH OF THE WOMEN

VISITING PARTY

HOME PARTY

forward. Finally the women finished in rear of their men, who thereupon broke into a peruperu or haka taparahi to which the visitors replied.

It can be seen therefore that any attempt to be dogmatic on this question of entrance is likely to cut across local tribal custom in one area or another. The important thing to note is that tradition can be found to support either a tama-tane or a tama-wahine approach and from either side of the stage or marae.

TENA RA KOUTOU KATOA

Here is a little welcome song which with suitable actions can make a simple but effective concert entrance.

Tena ra koutou katoa!	Greetings to you all!
Haere mai e nga. . .	We bid all people
Haere mai e nga iwi,	Welcome!
Tena ra koutou katoa!	Greetings to you all!
E te iwi, hui tonu ra;	O you people gathered here;
Tena ra koutou katoa!	Greetings to you all.
Mihi mai ra!	Greetings!
Mihi mai ra!	Yes, greetings!
Tena ra koutou katoa	Greetings to you all.

The group sings the little tune above as often as necessary while they side-step in their rows onto the stage. The hand action can be varied.

Once on stage with everyone in position the leader may then call 'Hope hei!' or 'Aue hei' to finish the introduction off. Then with everyone with hands on hips he will begin the action song which is to follow.

UTAINA MAI NGA WAKA

This is a more complex entrance embodying a number of actions. The words are by Kingi Ihaka. The tune, not reproduced here, is *Diana*.

Utaina mai nga waka,	Draw up the canoes
Nga waka o te motu,	The canoes of all the people,
Toia mai ra ki uta	Paddle towards the land
Ki te takotoranga,	Towards the place where it is to lie
Hikinuku, hiki e	Rise up from the waters
Hikirangi rangi e	Up on high
Tena, tena ra	Welcome greetings
Koutou katoa	Greetings to you all
Tena, tena ra	Welcome,
Koutou katoa!	Greetings to all!

Using the actions below, performers sidestep onto the stage. A sidestep is taken on each beat except for:

1st and 2nd lines: Sidestep on *first* beat only of the line.
Last line: No sidestep.

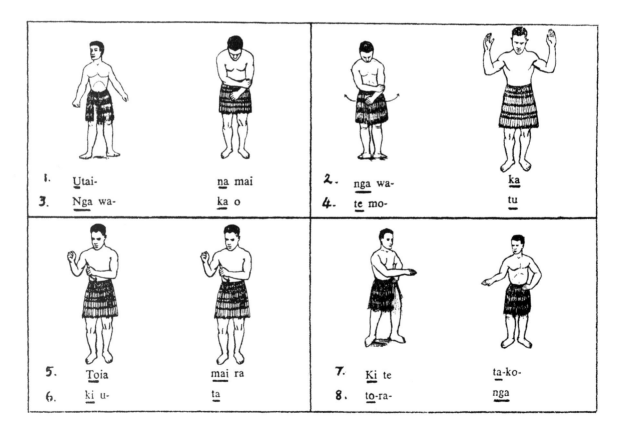

Hiki-   nuku   Hiki·   e

Hiki-   rangi   Rangi   e

Te............   (beat)
Na............   four times.   (beat)
Te............   na
Ra............   (beat)

Koutou   Katoa

HAKA ENTRANCES

The preceding are a little anaemic for haka entrances. Usually a chant is used to bring the party on. A popular one is:

Toia mai! Te waka!	Draw to the shore! The canoe!
Ki te urunga! Te waka!	To its rest! The canoe!
Ki te moenga! Te waka!	To its bed! The canoe!
Ki te takotoranga	To the place where it is to lie!
I takoto ai, te waka!	The canoe!

The action is simple. Something like those below on each beat of the chant.

From . . . . **To**

Often, however, a haka will not be staged until the group has been on stage for a time. It is therefore necessary to bring the men forward through the ranks of the women. This may be done in a great variety of ways. One is for the leader to give 'Hurihia' and then the men turn sideways with their right shoulders towards the audience. The leader then calls 'Nekeneke!' (move), and to a shout of 'Hei!' the men take one sidestep forward through the ranks of the women. The calls of 'Nekeneke!' and 'Hei!' are repeated as often as necessary to get the men into position. Another method is for the leader to call 'Toia mai' and on 'Te waka' the men take a short sideways hop forward, swinging the right foot up behind the left, at the same time hopping sideways on the left foot. This is repeated as often as necessary. Sometimes the short haka taparahi, *Ka mate* (chapter 19) can be used, with the men starting the haka from their position behind the women and, on the lines 'Tenei te tangata puhuruhuru' etc. moving forward through the women.

In chapter 16 a version of the taparahi *Poutini* is shown which can be used as a haka entrance.

PART TWO

MAORI GAMES

Introduction

The intention in this part of the book is to deal comprehensively with the mechanics of those Maori games which are still played in their traditional form (or something similar to it) by children. Maori games of old included kite flying, top spinning, a game similar to draughts and another like knucklebones, and sports such as running, jumping, swimming, boxing and wrestling. Although these pastimes had some features which were peculiar to the Maori, they had so many aspects in common with the games of generations of Pakeha children that they have only been covered briefly in chapter 5.

The sudden, tremendous upheaval of traditional ways caused by Pakeha civilization brought to an abrupt end the old leisured life. As the Maori began to cope — hesitantly at first and then with increasing confidence — with the demands imposed on them by the sudden impact of a new language and alien social and cultural usages, they also abandoned most of the ancient pastimes and amusements. This was further aggravated by the fact that many of the early missionaries possessed that perverted religious zeal, fashionable at the time, which saw evil in the unclothed bodies and innocent entertainment of indigenous peoples. Hence they instituted a policy which not only discouraged, but in some cases actively suppressed, the old Maori games. One elderly Maori told an early visitor, 'We are much puzzled by the new laws made for our people. We are not to spin humming tops on Sunday or peel kumara or potatoes . . .' A missionary writer describing Maori pastimes, mentioned with an air of satisfaction that '. . . amongst the missionary natives they [i.e. the pastimes] are entirely discontinued.'

Now the Maori have for the most part adopted either Pakeha amusements or else the Pakeha form of the games which they had played previously. Nevertheless there are three of the traditional Maori games which have survived and are still widely played to this day. These are the string games, which the Maori called 'whai' hand games, known by a variety of names, and stick games, for which the general name was 'ti rakau' but which are usually called today by the specific name of 'titi torea'. Each of these three games has a chapter to itself. They are simple to play, entertaining to watch, and easy to learn.

5

MAORI GAMES OF OLDEN TIMES

The Maori of old had no 'working week.' According to the pressure of circumstances they found time for games and other amusements. When preparing for battle, planting the crops or gathering the harvest there was no time for any frivolity. During the long evenings, however, or at the end of intensive periods of domestic activity, they relaxed and amused themselves in various ways. They had their important occasions and festivals when many days were devoted to games and competitions. Occasionally there would be an interchange of visits between villages for contests in such things as dancing, canoe racing, wrestling, etc. Many games and pastimes were similar to those found in other parts of Polynesia but some were distinctive to New Zealand.

The Whare Tapere

Most accounts of pre-European life mention the whare tapere or house of amusement, there are other Maori terms for it besides whare tapere. This, however, was in no sense a building set aside specifically for recreation. It is merely an all-embracing term for any house in which a group of people met for social purposes. In the summertime the village marae served as a whare tapere and as darkness fell, pitch-pine torches would be lit and cast their fiery glare over the merry scene.

Military Games

In Maoridom every citizen was a soldier and tribes were safe from marauders only because military prowess made them so. Therefore many games were designed to teach and foster the arts of war — as can be seen from an examination of

the games dealt with in the following chapters. Hand and stick games taught quickness of eye and reaction. Spear throwing was also popular. It taught the thrower accuracy and distance and for those who acted as a living target it taught agility in dodging, parrying and even catching the spear in mid-flight.

The various athletic sports, such as running, jumping, boxing and wrestling, also had a military value. Boxing with bare fists was principally a means of settling private arguments and was not widely used. Wrestling, however, was very important and was regarded as quite an art.

Water Sport

Swimming and diving, canoe racing and even surf riding were popular pastimes. Maori never dived into water head first but always feet first. Canoe racing was highly competitive between canoes belonging to different families or different tribes. Another aquatic pastime, morere, has a European equivalent called 'giant strides'. This was played from an apparatus consisting of a tall tree pole to which long vines were attached. The players grasped the vines and then swung around the pole in a large circle. Usually these poles were at the end of a drop into deep water and the players swung out over the water, let go and plummeted down. Shooting the surf took place either in small canoes or on a short plank.

Children's Games

Children, of course, played most of the livelong day. They played the games which would fit them to be warriors as well as many games with little practical value, but great amusement value. Kite flying was a firm favourite. Some of the more elaborate kites of considerable size were flown by men on a competitive basis. Sometimes kites were even used in an act of divination and various portents were drawn from their behaviour in the air. As can be expected from the popularity of surf riding on water, tobogganing down steep banks was popular on land. Mostly the toboggans were specially constructed, but other times they were merely a log or piece of wood. Similarly with stilt walking, sometimes the stilts were made for the task and sometimes an improvisation, such as a forked branch, was used. Piu or skipping was done in time to chanted jingles and in groups, with a number of people skipping at the same time over one rope. Maori children were very fond of top spinning. They used both whip tops, spun by winding the lash of a flaxen whip around the toy, and humming tops, which had a shaft projecting from the top around which the string was wound. Tops were made with wood, bone and even stone. Another game involved the use of hoops. These were spun along the ground by throwing. Another toy was called keretao. It was a small carved wooden figure with movable arms pulled by a cord. The toy was rather similar to a jumping jack. It was shaken up and down as the arms were pulled back and forth and looked for all the world as if it were dancing in time to the little jingles which the children sang.

TWO SIMPLE GAMES

MU TORERE

There are a number of minor games which Maori used to while away the long hours of leisure. One such game is mu torere. Some scholars claim that this is a post-contact game, and merely a variant of the game of draughts. The main basis for this theory seems to be the fact that 'mu' is also the Maori word for draughts and is a transliteration of the English word 'move'. However there seems to be no reason why a post-European word could

not have been applied to an ancient game, and since the game bears little resemblance to draughts other than the fact that objects are moved around a design, I am inclined to feel that this is a pre-European game.

Mu torere is played on the star-shaped design illustrated below.

Each player has four stones or counters, distinctively marked so that each can recognise his own. Player A puts his on the points 1, 2, 3, 4, Player B places his on the remaining points 5, 6, 7, 8.

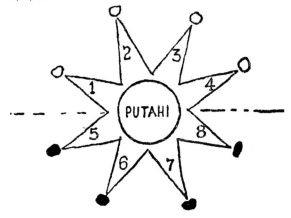

The rules of the game are:
(1) Players make a move alternately.
(2) Players may move a stone into the centre (putahi) or onto one of the points of the star, BUT only one stone is allowed on each point or on the centre at the same time.
(3) Players cannot jump over another stone but can only shift a stone to the centre or to the star point next to it.
(4) For the first two moves by either player, only the outer stones, that is the ones on 1, 4, 5, and 8, may be moved, for it is not permissible to block the other player in the first two moves.
(5) The game is won when one player is blocked by his opponent so that he is unable to move.

Illustrated below are various moves showing how a game of mu torere might be played. Player A has the white stones and player B has the black stones. It will be seen in the right-hand and diagram

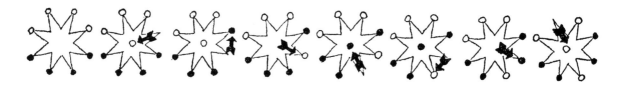

that player B is blocked, in that he is unable to move a stone to the centre or to an adjacent point. Hence player A has won the game.

KNUCKLEBONES

Another children's game of pre-European times which is still being played today is similar to the European game of knucklebones, and is played with small round stones or berries. Five is the number normally used, although early writers speak of skilled (adult) exponents having up to fifteen. Only the Ngati Porou East Coast version is known to me, but Elsdon Best records variants from Tuhoe and in the *Journal of the Polynesian Society* there is a Ngai Tahu version. It can be seen, of course, that the movements and methods of playing them are capable of many variations, and it must not be assumed that the sequences given below are the only ones played by the tribe named or are necessarily exclusive to it.

A Ngati Porou Version (called kai makamaka)
1st movement (korupu)
Four stones are laid in a square as below:

●   ●

●   ●

(a) The player throws the fifth stone in the air from the right hand and while it is airborne, scoops up another stone with the same hand, places it in the middle of the square, and then catches the fifth stone as it comes down.

(b) He repeats the above, each time moving another stone into the centre of the circle.

(c) Finally he throws the stone up again, and this time grabs up in his hand the four collected stones on the ground and, holding them in the right hand, catches the descending stone with the same hand.

2nd movement (korupu korua)
This is the same as the first movement, except that two stones instead of one are snatched up and placed into the centre each time that the fifth stone is thrown up.

3rd movement (huripapa)
All five stones are thrown up together and as many as possible caught on the back of the hand. If, for example, only two are caught, then the remaining three are piled together. One of the other stones is thrown up, and while it is in the air the other three are snatched up and the descending stone caught.

4th movement (kai makamaka)
(a) Four stones are placed out in a square. The fifth stone is thrown, a stone is snatched up from the ground by the throwing hand and then the fifth stone is caught as it falls.

(b) Now the two stones held are thrown up, another is snatched from the ground by the throwing hand and the two descending stones are caught.

(c) Then the three are thrown up, another is snatched up and the three falling stones caught.

(d) Finally four stones are thrown up, the fifth is snatched up and the four falling stones caught. Thus all five are now held in the hand.

A Tuhoe Version (called ruru)

For this game one stone is marked distinctively and called 'hai'. It is the principal stone. The others are the 'kaimahi' or workmen.

Preliminary

All five stones are thrown up, and as many as possible are caught as they fall, on the back of the hand.

1st movement (takitahi)

The hai is thrown by the right hand. While it is in flight one of the kaimahi is snatched up by the right hand then the same hand catches the hai as it falls. This is repeated, with another stone being grabbed from the ground each time until all five stones are held.

2nd movement (takirua)

This is as for the first movement except that two kaimahi stones are snatched up each time with the right hand.

3rd movement (takitoru)

This time as the hai is thrown, three kaimahi must be snatched up before the hai falls and is caught.

4th movement (takiwha)

Four kaimahi stones must be snatched up together for this movement.

5th movement (poipoi)

A stick is laid along the ground in front of the player and pointing away from him. One stone is placed on the left side of this stick and the other stone opposite on the right side.

(a) The hai is thrown with the right hand, then this hand snatches up the stone to the right of the stick and throws it up.

(b) While this latter stone is airborne, the player catches the falling hai and throws it up again.

(c) Meanwhile the descending kaimahi is caught in the left hand and thrown up again.

(d) The left hand then snatches up the stone left of the stick and throws it up. This left-hand stone is caught by the right hand as it falls while the left hand catches the hai and the other kaimahi.

6th movement (koropu)

A small circle is marked on the ground and the hai and three kaimahi arranged equal distant around its circumference. All throwing and catching is with the right hand.

(a) The hai is thrown up and while it is airborne the other three stones are moved to the centre by the right hand so that they are touching. The falling hai is then caught.

(b) The hai is thrown again and before it is caught the three stones must be grabbed up by the throwing hand.

Final movement (ruru — meaning close together)

Three kaimahi are placed touching one another.

(a) The hai is thrown with the right hand and before being caught, a kaimahi is grabbed up and thrown with the same hand.

(b) The right hand catches the hai and throws it again.

(c) The left hand catches the kaimahi and holds it.

(d) Before the falling hai is caught and while in fact (c) is taking place, the right hand grabs a second kaimahi and throws it. This second kaimahi is also caught and held in the left hand.

(e) Meanwhile hai is caught with the right hand and thrown yet again. While airborne, a third kaimahi is snatched up by the right hand and thrown.

(f) Finally the hai is caught and held in the right hand while the third kaimahi is caught and held, along with its mates, in the left hand.

To add a twist to this most difficult movement, should any of the kamahi move (remember they are on the ground touching one another) when one of its companions is scooped up, the player has failed and must start again.

A Ngai Tahu Version (called koruru)

1st movement (paka or panga)

Four stones are placed on the ground in pairs.

(a) The fifth stone is thrown with the right hand and the same hand picks up two stones then catches the falling fifth stone.

(b) Holding the first two stones still in the right hand, the fifth stone is thrown again and the remaining two stones are scooped up.

2nd movement (takitoru)

Four stones are placed on the ground

(a) One of the four is thrown and while airborne the other three are snatched up.

(b) Repeat.

3rd movement (takiwha)

One stone is thrown and while airborne the other four are scooped up with the throwing hand.

4th movement (koriwha)

Four stones are held in the hand.

(a) Throw up one and catch it, throw the same stone and catch it again.

(b) Put the four stones on the ground and do the paka (first) movement again.

5th movement (raraki — this is South Island dialect for rarangi)

Four stones are placed in a square.

One stone is thrown up four times. Each time as it is airborne the throwing hand quickly scoops up one of the four stones on the ground and places it to the middle of the square before catching the thrown stone. Finally the four stones are scooped up together while the fifth is airborne.

6th movement (piu)

Begin with all five stones in the hand. Throw up one, place the other four out in a square, and catch the falling stone.

7th movement (huri)

Throw all five and catch all on the back of the hand. This should be continued until all five are caught.

8th movement (koruru)

Leave one stone on the ground and retain four in the right hand. Throw the four up, pick up the fifth, catch the four as they fall.

Although I have classed knucklebones as a child's game, it was often played competitively by adults, individually and in the family and village teams. Played in this way, teams usually consisted of between two and ten players. The competition could be organised in different ways. All could start on a signal and the winner would be the team or individual who first completed all movements correctly. In the event of a player making a mistake, he would either have to return to the very beginning or continue the movement until he did it correctly. Another method, suitable for individual competition, was for players to take turns. A change took place whenever a player made a mistake. He who finished all figures first or who had progressed the furthest in a given time was declared the winner.

6

HAND GAMES (MAHI RINGARINGA)

There was a dual purpose to hand games as they were practised by the Maori of old. Not only were they a social amusement to while away leisure hours in harmless fun but they also inculcated a quickness of eye and reaction most necessary for the warrior .

Most hand games are played between two people although some can be played by a larger group. They consist of a rapid series of actions made by the hands and arms in time to a chanted call. Naturally there was considerable variation in calling and actions between various tribes. Nowadays the games have become fairly stereotyped but anyone with imagination can devise a number of variations on the movements described below.

GENERAL RULES

Method of Play

(1) The game begins with the two players facing one another. They then play a number of rounds. Some games start each round with one of the players issuing a kind of challenge, to which the other player replies. In other games the round begins with the first call. We shall call the person who makes the first call of a round the *caller*.

(2) Each round consists of a number of rapid hand and/or body movements made by the players.

(3) For each movement one of the players makes a call as he makes the movement. Simultaneously the other player (whom we shall call the *follower*) also makes a move but says nothing.

(4) For the next movement, the second player (who was the follower in the previous movement) now gives the call, while his partner (who was the caller in the previous movement) says nothing.

(5) So the round continues in a series of moves with each player taking it in turn to be the caller.

Winning a Round

(1) A round is won when the follower makes exactly the same movement simultaneously with the caller.

(2) If this happens the caller must shout 'ra' at the end of his call. If he manages to do this immediately, then he wins the round. (See below for the system of scoring.)

(3) If the caller does not manage to shout 'ra' before the other player starts the next call then he has missed his chance and the game continues.

(4) If there is any dispute about whether the caller managed to shout 'ra' in time (and in a fast-moving game, there often is doubt), then either player may call for a proving round, which decides who won the disputed round.

Scoring

There are two methods of scoring used.

(1) Whoever wins the round takes the point and starts the next round, OR

(2) If the caller wins, he takes a point and starts the next round. It the other player wins he scores nothing but merely earns the right to start the new round. In so doing, of course, he becomes the caller, and if he wins the new round he will earn a point as well as continuing in the role of caller until such time as he loses.

Most games involve a running score in Maori

and the first player to win a given number of rounds wins the game. The Maori numerals are:

1 = tahi	2 = rua	3 = toru
4 = wha	5 = rima	6 = ono
7 = whitu	8 = waru	9 = iwa
	10 = tekau	

1 — HIPITOI

This is a very simple game and is best for the beginner to cut his teeth on.

Positions
The elbows are held in against the sides with the forearms parallel to the ground. The hands make the following movements.

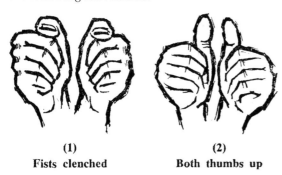

| **(1)** | **(2)** |
| Fists clenched | Both thumbs up |

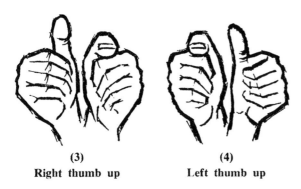

| **(3)** | **(4)** |
| Right thumb up | Left thumb up |

Calling
(a) Sometimes the caller starts the game by calling 'hipitoi' and the other answers 'ae'. Then the game progresses as follows.

(b) Usually however the game commences with the caller making the first action and calling 'hipitoi' and this is called by each player as he makes his subsequent actions.

(c) When one player catches the other, he calls 'hipitoitoi ra!'

(d) The winner of the first point begins his second round by calling 'rua hipitoi'

and so on.

Scoring
Each player keeps his own score. After winning a round, the winner initiates the next round with the next highest number (for him). For example, let us assume in a particular game that player A has won four rounds and player B has won two rounds. If player A wins a round he will start off his next round by 'rima (five) hipitoi'. If, however, player B wins it, his next call will instead be 'toru hipitoi'. The first player to reach and win the tenth round wins the game. In the Arawa version of the game, however, the first player to reach and win the tenth round must be two clear rounds ahead of his opponent before he can claim to have won the game.

2 — HEI TAMA TU TAMA

This is another good game, although harder than hipitoi and quite tiring if played with speed and vigour and with a swaying body movement.

Positions
This game is played with arm instead of hand movements. There are four basic positions, from which experienced players may evolve variations. In some versions of the game, positions 3 and 4 can be reversed once only, and then either positions 1 or 2 must be used before 3 or 4 can be used again.

Calling
(a) The game begins with both players adopting position 1. One challenges the other with the call 'Hei tama tu tama!' and the other accepts by calling

38

'Ae!' (yes).

(b) The challenger then goes into his first movement. As each action is made the player calls 'Hei tama tu tama!'

(c) The winner of a round starts the next round with his next highest number — 'Toru hei tama tu tama!' or whatever it may be.

Note: (a) is often omitted and the game begins with the starter going directly into his first movement.

Scoring

The method of scoring is the same as for hipitoi.

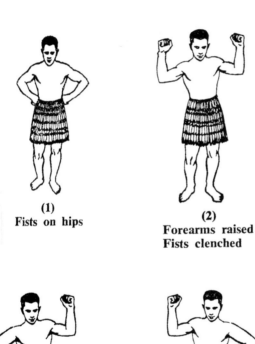

(1)
Fists on hips

(2)
Forearms raised
Fists clenched

(3)
(4)
One fist raised
Other fist on hip

3 — TAMA TAMA TU TAMA

This is an Arawa hand game which is very similar to Hei Tama Tu Tama.

Positions

Again there are four basic movements capable of variation by good players.

(1) Hands slapped on upper legs; (2) forearms both raised, hands open and level with the ears; (3) and (4) one arm raised with fist clenched, elbow slapped with other hand.

The players crouch forward slightly from the waist and obtain rhythm by swaying the hips.

In some versions of the game, positions 3 and 4 may be reversed only once and then either positions 1 or 2 must be used before 3 or 4 can be used again.

(1)
Hands slapped on
upper legs

(2)
Forearms both raised
Hands open and level
with the ears

(3)
(4)
One arm raised with fist clenched
Elbow slapped with other hand

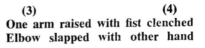

Calling

(a)   One player challenges the other with 'Tama tama tu tama' and the latter replies 'Tama tu tama.' Both set the rhythm as they call by slapping their thighs in position 1.

(b)   Players call 'Tama tu tama' with each action.

(c)   When one player catches out the other he must call 'Tama tu tama RA!'

Scoring

As for hipitoi.

4 — WHAKAROPIROPI OR HOMAI

This is one of the most complex and lively of all the Maori hand games and probably the best known, being popular all over New Zealand. It is quite difficult, needing considerable practice to do properly, and it is very fascinating to watch. The game is known by a variety of names — 'Ti ringa' in the North, 'Matimati' among the Tuhoe and Te Arawa, 'Ku' is the East Coast variation, Elsdon Best records the name 'Hikawai' from Gisborne, and also 'Pokirua', but the most common names are 'Whakaropiropi' or 'Homai'.

Positions

There are two sets of movements for Whakaropiropi. One set consists of arm movements and the other of hand movements. Sometimes players use only one set or the other but skilful exponents usually run the whole gamut of positions in the course of a round. During the game, performers adopt a half-crouching stance. To begin with, they may be about a metre apart, and as the excitement of a hotly contested round grows they move closer and closer until the point is taken with fierce grimaces and war cries.

A — ARM MOVEMENTS

(1)
Hands beat on upper legs

(2)
Open hands at ear level

(3)   **(4)**
Both hands extended to one side of the body
Hands open and below waist

(5)
Hands on chest

(1)
Both fists closed
Elbows into sides

(2)
Elbows into sides
Forearms parallel to the
ground and extending
straight out from body
Hands open

(3)
As for (2) but fingertips
touching

(4)
Right hand open and
held over left, resting in
the gap between thumb
and forefinger
(Left thumb is in the
palm of right hand)

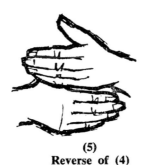

(5)
Reverse of (4)

(6)
The reverse of (3), i.e.,
the wrists touching and
the hands forming a V
open at the tips of the
fingers

Calling

The calling for whakaropiropi is more complex than the proceeding games.

(a) *To begin:*

Caller challenges: 'Whakaropiropi ai?' (shall we play whakaropiropi?)

Follower replies 'Ae!' (yes)

Caller (making first move) 'Tenei mea te homai' (this is my move)

For the first two calls, that is, the challenge and the reply, the hands are beaten on the thighs in movement 1. The game then begins and on each action the caller calls 'Homai!'

(b) *On one player catching the other out:*

As with the other games, the aim is for the caller to catch the follower making the same action simultaneously. When he catches him, however, he must call 'Homai ra!' before the other takes up the call or the round continues.

(c) *On the first round being won:*

The next round starts off as follows. The winner of the first round calls first.

Winner: 'Tahi ra ano' (or 'Kei te tahi nei ano' — that is the first point)

Loser: 'Koe' (short for 'I a koe' — to you), OR 'Ae' (Agreed!).

Winner: 'Tenei mea te homai!' (he makes his first move of the new round as he calls this)

Loser: 'Homai!' etc.

For the first two calls, the beat is set again by reverting to the first movement. Then on 'Tenei mea te homai' the player makes his action.

(d) *On the winner of a round being disputed*:

If the winning of a round is disputed, a proving round is held to decide the point. He who claims to be the winner calls as follows.

Claimant: 'Puruwha ra ano' (Puruwha is merely a transliteration of the word proof, the meaning being 'Let us prove the point').

Other: 'Ae!'

Claimant: 'Tenei me mea te homai!'

Other: 'Homai!' etc.

Scoring

As with the other games, each player keeps his own score and, if he wins a point, starts off the next round by calling his score to date, e.g. 'Tahi ra ano,' 'Rua ra ano,' 'Toru ra ano,' etc. This continues until they reach iwa (nine). The player who wins the ninth round calls 'Piro ra ano!' This is short for 'Kei te piro nei ano', and he is thus saying, 'This is my winning round' for 'piro' in Maori means 'out' when referring to games.

Let us assume that player A is up to his 'piro' or winning round, and that player B has so far won only six rounds. Player A now loses his 'piro' round. Player B as the winner, starts the next round with the call 'Ono ra ano!' (In other words, 'That was my sixth point'.) Even if player A now wins this round, he has still not won the game. He must start off the new round with 'Piro ra ano' and will not win the game until he has won a 'piro' round.

When Arawa children play Whakaropiropi, the principle of winning the piro round is the same, except that it does not come after the ninth round. From iwa, the call is:

10 ='Mate ra ano' (Kei te mate nei ano).

11 = 'Heke ra ano' (Kei te heke nei ano).

OUT = 'Piro ra ano' (Kei te piro nei ano).

5 — OTHER VERSIONS OF WHAKAROPIROPI

Ti Ringa

This is played in North Auckland. The movements are similar to Whakaropiropi. When a player has won a round, he keeps repeating 'Ti tahi, ti tahi, ti tahi' until he wins a second round, when he calls 'Ti rua' and so on up to 'Ti ngahuru' (ten).

E Ropi

The actions are the same as Whakaropiropi. The round begins with each player having his hands behind his back. The caller calls 'Eeeee ropi!' and brings his arms out into one of the movements. His opponent watches him closely and forfeits a point if he does not bring his hands out simultaneously. Of course, the caller tries to trick his opponent into bringing his hands out too quickly or to slowly by prolonging the initial 'e'. The progressive count is 'Tahi ropi!', 'Rua ropi!' etc. Once a round has begun it continues as in Whakaropiropi, except that 'ropi' replaces 'homai' as the call.

Hakiparepare (Also known as 'Hokoparepare')

This version incorporates only the arm movements of Whakaropiropi. The first round begins with the caller putting his hands on his thighs in position 1 and calling out 'Hakiparepare'. The follower carries out the same action and replies 'Anaparepare'. The leader again calls 'Hakiparepare', both continuing the first movement on 'haki' and assuming one of the other positions on 'pare'. If the follower carries out the same action as the caller, he has won the round, and initiates the next round by calling 'Tahi hakiparepare'. The tahi is long drawn out to re-establish the rhythm, and, as before, the movement is made on the 'pare'. The subsequent rounds begin with the winner of the previous round calling out his score, 'rua hakiparepare' 'toru hakiparepare' or whatever it might be.

6 — MATIMATI

This is also a hand game which requires considerable skill and practice. It is found in the Mataatua district and played by both Tuhoe and Te Arawa. It is also known in other parts of Polynesia. It is only to be expected, a number of variations have grown up of which the version which follows is only one.

Positions and Calling

The players face one another then call out a little jingle, such as the one given below, while at the same time establishing the rhythm by clapping the hands together or on the thighs.

Matimati

E mati ra

E toru nawa

Te ngiono, whitu, waru

Te iwa haka tuku mai.

Both players then go rapidly through the actions in the following sequence:

'Matimati': Clap clenched fists together.

'Tahi matimati': Clap open hands together.

'Rua matimati': Hands open, fingers extended, right thumb struck across left thumb.

'Toru matimati': Right fist clenched and struck on open palm of left hand.

'Wha matimati': Two open hands are brought together and the fingers interlocked.

'Rima matimati': Thumb of right hand pushed between first and second fingers of left hand, right hand fingers pointing upwards.

'Ono matimati': Clap clenched fists together.

'Whitu matimati': Hands opened, fingers extended, right thumb struck across left thumb.

'Waru matimati': Hands open. Clap hands but with the heels of the palm only making contact with each other.

'Iwi matimati': Clap clenched fists together.

'Piro matimati': Open right hand strikes on the palm of the left hand.

Scoring

When players are going through the sequence all the movements must be made correctly, simultaneously and at maximum speed. If one player falls behind or makes an incorrect movement, his opponent takes the point and the round starts again. The player who wins the most out of ten rounds wins the game.

7 — MATE RAWA

Although popular elsewhere, this is an Arawa hand game, and probably requires the most practice of all since not only the actions but also the calling have to be learned and mastered.

Positions

The five given below are the basic positions.

(1)
Hands beat on upper legs

(2)
Hands and arms inclined to right
Palm of right hand and back of left facing front

(3)
Reverse of (2)

43

(4)
**Hands open and
opposite ears**

(5)
Hands on chest

These can be made into double actions, with one player tricking the other by pretending to go to one position and then changing quickly to his opponent's position. Other than this, however, the game must progress to a new action each call.

Note: A Nga Puhi version of this game uses the hand movements of 'Whakaropiropi' instead of the movements given above.

Calling

In mate rawa, special calls are used instead of the Maori numerals common in other games.

Mate rawa

Toro rawa

Ngihi ono

Whitu waru

Te iwa haka

Tuku mai

Kumate (a corruption of 'kua mate')

To Begin the Game

Player A is the caller and calls: 'Mate rawa mate rawa'. Both players beat hands on thighs as position 1

Player B answers 'E mate e mate!' Both players simultaneously make a movement.

Player A calls 'E mate!'

Both players make a movement.

Player B calls 'E mate!'

Both players make a movement.

Player A calls 'E mate!'

Both players make a movement.

Player B calls 'E mate!'

Both players make a movement.

And so on. The round is won when both players make the same movement simultaneously. The winner is the player who was caller for the particular movement.

To Begin the Next Round

Caller calls: 'Toro rawa, toro rawa!'

Both players action 1.

Other player answers: 'E toro, e toro!'

Both players action 1.

Caller calls: 'E toro!'

Players make a movement.

Other player calls: 'E toro!'

Players make a movement.

('E toro' is called on each movement until the point is won. Then the next round is begun with 'Ngihi ono'. The repy is 'E ngihi, e ngihi!' So the game continues through to kumate).

Scoring

Unlike 'Whakaropiropi' there is no winning call such as 'Homai Ra'. The rounds are numbered through consecutively from mate to kumate, irrespective of who wins the point. In other words, the call for each round is NOT the winner of the previous round's score of how many rounds he has won. The winner of the game is the player who wins the largest number of rounds out of seven.

7
STICK GAMES (TI RAKAU)

Once again this is a game which is strongly rythmical and obviously designed to practise dexterity of hand and quickness of eye. The form of the game, and even its name, differ from tribe to tribe. Although today it is usually played, in very simple form, mainly by women, in days of old it was a serious war game. The Ngati Porou version was called poi rakau and the players stood in a circle, except for one, who remained in the centre of the circle. Each person in the circle had a light stick around 900cm long. Watched by an umpire who ensured fair throwing, the players threw their rods at the centre player, who had to catch them and throw them back to their owner. If he missed, the person who had thrown the stick took his place. All this was done in time to a song but, as can be appreciated, practice at this made the catching of a spear in battle much easier. Another version involved players standing in two ranks facing one another approximately three metres apart. One stick only was thrown back and forth and any player who missed had to retire, until only the victor was left. In the well-known Arawa version of the game, the players kneel in a circle and the game proceeds to music. Sometimes some of the players are without sticks and catch those thrown to them by players who have sticks. In other games each player throws his right-hand stick and with the same hand catches the incoming stick.

There is some doubt about the correct Maori terminology for stick games. Ti is the name of a mythological type of tree, which was reputed to appear to change its position as if by magic. The discovery of one of these trees in the bush was reputed to be an evil omen. It will be appreciated how a word denoting trees which changed position came to be applied to games involving the throwing of sticks. Usually 'ti rakau' is used today to denote stick games generally, although

one authority says it was a game played by the feet. This must, however, be somewhat suspect. The term titi is used for the short sticks used in ti rakau. Another popular name for all stick games is titi torea, which is a corruption of titi-to-ure. This term must, however, be regarded as a vulgarism and probably applied originally to a specific game.

The Sticks
In old versions of the game the sticks were more like spears, and up to 90cm in length. Today they are often as short as 30cm, but sticks as short as this are easily dropped and 45 to 50cm long sticks are recommended, with a diameter of 2.5cm. They may be painted, carved or have burnt-in designs. Brightly painted sticks give the best effect for public performances.

Throwing the Sticks
Many novices make the mistake of worrying about what happens to their own sticks once they are thrown, whereas it is essential that they concentrate on the sticks they have to catch. The sticks should be thrown with a lobbing motion as this makes them easier to catch. The sticks must be held lightly with the thumb on one side and the finger-tips on the other, not clasped in the fists. Each player arranges with his partner so that for the throwing movements one throws more to the left and the other more to the right to avoid mid-air collisions. One set of movements at a time should be mastered before attempting anything more and a novice should carry out the movements slowly but to a strict beat.

The Music
Any music in 3/4 or 6/8 time is suitable. Often a chant is used. However, the tunes following are the ones most usually performed with stick games.

E Aue!

E aue! Ka mate au!   Alas! The pain will kill me.
E hine, hoki iho ra.   Oh! Maiden return to me.

E Papa Waiari

E papa waiari   Sighing and grieving
Taku nei mahi   Is what I have been doing
Taku nei mahi   Is what I have been doing
He tuku roimata.   Here are my tears of woe.

Maku e!

Maku e kaute o hikoitanga   I will count your footsteps
Maku e kaute o hikoitanga   Yes count your footsteps

Hurihuri

Hurihuri, hurihuri o mahara e   Your thoughts are ever turning
Ki te tau, ki te tau, ki te tau e.   Towards your beloved
Kore, rawa, kore rawa e mahara e.   Yet not a thought is spared
Ki a koe ra, e hine.   For you, my love!

TITI TOREA — PLAYERS IN PAIRS

Form of the Games

The version of ti rakau given below is called titi torea and is carried out with the performers in pairs opposite one another, kneeling with the buttocks resting on the heels and the backs straight. When practising for prolonged periods performers should sit or kneel on a cushion. The former is recommended as the kneeling position can be very tiring at first.

The game consists of a number of sets done to the tune 'E Papa' or 'Maku e'. Each set is interspersed with a chorus to the tune 'E Aue!' The chorus is equivalent to marking time and gives performers time to pick up dropped sticks and generally prepare themselves for the next set. The game finishes with a very quick set of movements done to the tune 'Hurihuri'. Although the sets of movements given below have been numbered consecutively, there is in fact no particular order in which the sets should follow one another, although it is usual to progress from the simple to the more complex. There are, of course, variations to the movements given below and players can make up their own as they go along.

Initially the sticks are laid on the ground in front of the players as shown above. On the command 'kia rite' (be ready) the sticks are picked up and brought to the ready position shown in the illustration on the top right of this page. As the sticks come to the vertical they are rapped on the ground. The leader gives 'toru wha' and the chorus begins, followed by the first set, then a chorus followed by another set, and so on. Each movement occupies one beat of the music, except where sticks are tapped twice or flipped twice, in which case each tap or flip takes one beat.

CHORUS (Tune *E Aue!*)

There are three movements, each one carried out on the first, second and third beats of the bar respectively.

Movement 1

Sticks are rapped on the ground from the vertical position.

Movement 2

Each player knocks his own sticks together.

Movement 3

Each player knocks his sticks against those of his partner.

There is also an alternative set of three movements which can be used for the chorus.

Movement 1A
LEFT stick held about 14cm off the ground. RIGHT stick tapped on ground.

Movement 2A
Each player flips his RIGHT stick so that he catches it by the opposite end.

Movement 3A
RIGHT stick tapped against partner's RIGHT stick.

SET NO. 1 — THE SINGLE THROW
(Tune E Papa)

There are three movements which are continued over and over again until the tune finishes.

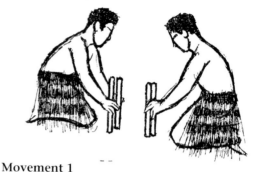

Movement 1
Sticks are tapped on the ground.

Movement 2
Each player knocks his own sticks together.

Movement 3
Each player throws his RIGHT stick to his partner and with his RIGHT hand catches his partner's stick.

Movements 1 and 2 are then repeated and then movement 3 but this time it is the LEFT stick which is thrown instead of the RIGHT.

SET NO. 2 — THE DOUBLE THROW
(Tune *E Papa*)

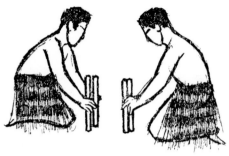

Movement 1
Sticks are tapped on the ground.

Movement 2
Sticks are tapped together.

Movement 3
Player throws his RIGHT stick to his partner and catches the partner's RIGHT stick.

Movement 4
Player throws his LEFT stick to his partner and catches at the same time the partner's LEFT stick.

SET NO. 3 — DOUBLE DOUBLE THROW
(Tune *E Papa*)

This consists of six movements and is merely an extension of set no. 2.

Movements 1 to 4
As for set no. 2.

Movement 5 and 6
Movements 3 and 4 of set no. 2 repeated.

SET NO. 4 — A DOUBLE THROW
(Tune *E Papa*)

There are four movements to this set. Throwing the sticks in the manner laid down for this and the following set demands much more dexterity and quickness than for the previous three sets.

Movements 1 and 2
As for previous sets.

Movement 3
Player A throws his RIGHT stick and catches B's stick in his RIGHT hand while at the same time B throws his LEFT stick and catches A's stick in his left hand.

Movement 4
Player A throws his LEFT stick and catches B's stick in his LEFT hand while at the same time B throws his RIGHT stick and catches A's stick in his RIGHT hand.

SET NO. 5 — A DOUBLE DOUBLE THROW
(Tune *E Papa*)

Movements 1 to 4
As for set no. 4.

Movement 5 and 6
Movement 3 and 4 of set no. 4 repeated.

SET NO. 6 — IN AND OUT
(Tune *Maku e*)

Movements 1 and 2
As for previous sets.

(a)
One player holds his sticks apart

(b)
The other player holds his sticks together

Movement 3

Each player throws both this sticks together and catches those of his partner. When they throw, one set of sticks pass between the other.

SET NO. 7 — THE FLIP
(Tune *E Papa*)

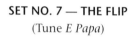

Movement 1

Sticks tapped on the ground on the player's RIGHT

Movement 2

Both sticks are flipped over and the other ends caught.

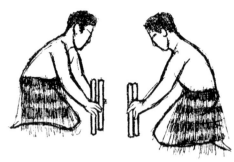

Movement 3

Sticks tapped on ground.

Movement 4

Sticks tapped together.

Movements 5 and 6

As for movements 3 and 4 of set no. 2.

FINAL SET — HURIHURI
(Tune *Hurihuri*)

Hurihuri concludes the game after the final chorus. It is taken at a considerably faster tempo than the other tunes and if no sticks are dropped makes a spectacular finish.

Movement 1 (1 bar)
Sticks tapped on the player's RIGHT side.

Movement 2 (1 bar)
Both sticks are flipped TWICE.

Movement 3 (1 beat)
Sticks tapped on the ground.

Movement 4 (1 beat)
Sticks tapped together.

Movement 5 (2 beats)
Each player taps his RIGHT stick twice against his partner's RIGHT stick.

The above series of movements are repeated again twice. The only difference is that for the first repeat the sticks are tapped on the LEFT side for position 1 and it is the LEFT sticks which are tapped in movement 5. For the second repeat it is as above, followed by:

Movement 6 (2 bars)
Sticks flipped twice.

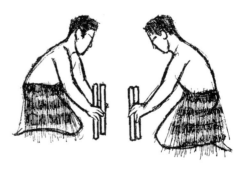

Movement 7 (1 beat)
Sticks tapped on ground.

Movement 8 (1 beat)
Sticks tapped together.

Movement 9 (1 beat)
Sticks placed together on the ground with a bang.

PLAYERS IN GROUPS OF FOUR

Some of the foregoing movements may be performed by players in groups of four. In effect, the players work in two pairs, one of the pairs inserting extra beats into their opening movement of each set to ensure that, when they throw, their sticks do not collide in mid-air with the sticks of the other pair.

Chorus 'E Aue'

This set is the same as before, except that for the third movement, each player taps his LEFT stick against the RIGHT stick of his neighbour and his RIGHT stick against the neighbour's LEFT.

SET NO. 1 — THE SINGLE THROW IN FOURS
(Tune *E Papa*)

This is done in the same way as set no. 1 for pairs, except that, to ensure synchronisation, one pair for their very first position only give their sticks two taps on the ground instead of one. The other pair continue as normal. The progress of the set and effect of the extra tap is best shown by the chart below.

(a) Chorus, *E Aue*
(b) Tap sticks once on ground (fig. 1)
(c) Tap sticks again on ground (fig 1)
(d) Tap sticks together (fig.2)
(e) Throw RIGHT stick to partner opposite (fig. 3)
(f) Tap stick on ground
(g) Tap sticks together
(h) Throw LEFT stick to partner
(I) Tap sticks on ground
(j) Tap sticks together and so on.

2nd Pair

(a) Chorus, *E Aue*
(b) Tap sticks once on ground (fig. 1)
(c) Tap sticks together (fig. 2)
(d) Throw RIGHT stick to partner opposite (fig. 3)
(e) Tap stick on ground
(f) Tap sticks together

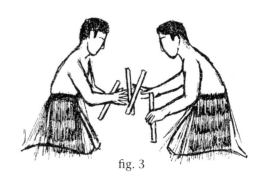

fig. 1   fig. 2   fig. 3

(g) Throw left stick to partner
(h) Tap sticks on ground
(i) Tap sticks together
(j) Throw RIGHT stick to partner.

The effect of the extra beat created by movement (c) ensures that only one pair at a time are actually throwing their sticks.

SET NO. 2 — THE DOUBLE THROW IN FOURS
(Tune *E Papa*)

Again the only difference from the set in pairs is a matter of extra beats inserted to ensure synchronisation. One pair, *again for the first time only,* give their sticks *three* taps on the ground. The sequence is:

(h) Tap sticks on ground
(I) Tap sticks together
(j) Throw RIGHT stick
(k) Throw LEFT stick and so on.

2nd Pair
(a) Chorus *E Aue*
(b) Tap sticks on ground (fig. 1)
(c) Tap sticks together (fig. 2)
(d) Throw RIGHT stick to partner and catch (fig. 3)
(e) Throw LEFT stick to partner and catch
(f) Tap sticks on ground
(g) Tap sticks together
(h) Throw RIGHT stick
(I) Tap sticks on ground
(k) Tap sticks together.

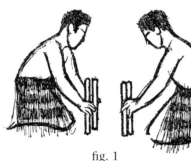   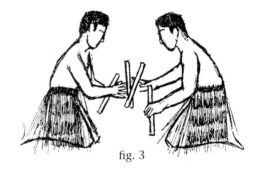

fig. 1   fig. 2   fig. 3

1st Pair
(a) Chorus *E Aue*
(b) Tap sticks on ground (fig. 1)
(c) Tap sticks again on ground
(d) Tap sticks again on ground
(e) Tap sticks together (fig. 2)
(f) Throw RIGHT stick to partner and catch (fig. 3).
(g) Throw LEFT stick to partner and catch

SET NO. 3 — THE IN AND OUT IN FOURS
(Tune *Maku e*)

The movement itself is unchanged. (See set no. 6 of titi torea in pairs.) Synchronisation is achieved in the same way as for the first set above — namely, one pair give their sticks two taps initially on the ground instead of one.

STICK GAME PLAYERS IN ROWS

The version of ti rakau which follows is often considered more suitable for concert purposes than titi torea, because all players kneel in a long row facing the audience, and thus all movement of the sticks can be clearly seen. To begin, only the leader, who is the person in the centre of the row, has sticks, and the opening movement consists of passing out of the sticks to the other performers. Five movements then follow, and then there is a closing movement in which all sticks are passed back to the leader. This game stands or falls on the stick handling ability of the person acting as leader.

OPENING MOVEMENT — PASSING OUT THE STICKS
(Tune *E Papa*)

(b)   **(a)**   **Leader**   **(a)**   **(b)**

1. The performers kneel in a row (or a circle), with the leader in the centre with all the sticks in a heap before him (or her).

2. On 'Kia rite' the leader picks up two sticks as shown, while the remainder assume either the hope position or with the hands resting lightly on the upper leg.

(b)   **(a)**   **Leader**   **(a)**   **(b)**

3. On the first beat of the bar the leader throws his stick to the performer on either side (performer a).

4. The performer on each side catches the stick with the hand farthest away from the leader i.e. the OUTSIDE hand. Remaining performers sit still and sing.

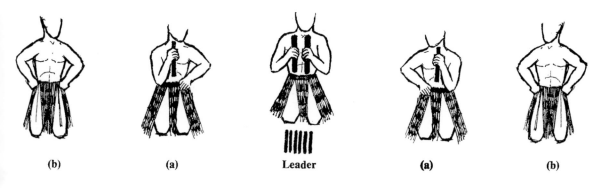

(b) (a) Leader (a) (b)

5. On the remaining beats of the bar, the leader picks up another two sticks and makes ready to throw.

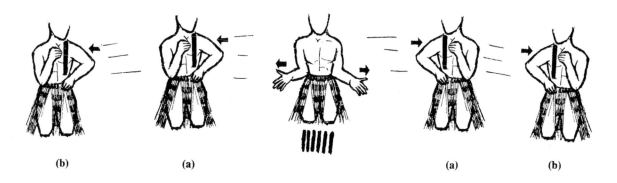

(b) (a) (a) (b)

6. On the first beat of the next bar, the leader throws another stick out to the performers on his left and right (a).

7. Simultaneously these performers throw the sticks that they have been holding out to the performers (b) beside them. This continues on the first beat of each bar until all performers are holding a stick in their OUTSIDE hand. The secret of throwing a stick and at the same time catching one is for all performers to look inwards and to concentrate on the stick which is being thrown to them, and not to worry whether the stick which they have just thrown is caught by the next neighbour.

Alternative

As an alternative to the above.

(a) The leader picks up two sticks and taps them on the floor on the *first* beat of the bar.

(b) He taps them together (fig. 2, page 53) in the air on the *second* beat

(c) He throws them outwards on the *third* beat (as illustrated above). This continues until all sticks are distributed. The other performers, as they get sticks, follow the leader's movements and throw on the third beat of each bar.

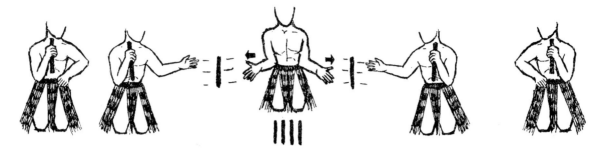

8. When all players have a stick in their outside hand they catch the sticks which the leader is throwing in their inside hand until all performers have two sticks each.

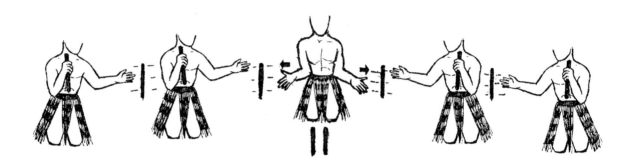

MARKING TIME

Once the sticks are distributed, there is a 'marking time' movement to the tune *E Aue* to give the performers time to settle down before movement 1 begins.

Tap on ground

Beat 1
Beat 4, etc.

Tap together

Beat 2
Beat 5, etc.

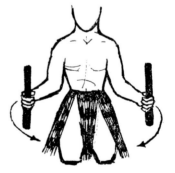

Carry sticks out from body and then in again for tap on ground for beat 4

Beat 3
Beat 6, etc.

FIRST MOVEMENT
(Tune, last 8 bars of *E Papa*)

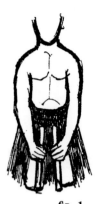

fig. 1

Sticks tapped on floor

Beat 1
Beat 7
Beat 13
Beat 19

fig. 2

Sticks tapped on floor

Beat 2
Beat 8
Beat 14
Beat 20

fig. 3

Sticks flipped

Beat 3
Beat 9
Beat 15
Beat 21

fig. 4

Sticks tapped on floor

Beat 4
Beat 10
Beat 16
Last bar

fig. 5

Sticks thrown to opposite hands

Beat 5
Beat 11
Beat 17

fig. 6

Sticks thrown to opposite hands

Beat 6
Beat 12
Beat 18

For figures 5 and 6 left stick is thrown and caught in right hand. Simultaneously right stick thrown across and caught in left hand. This is done twice each time i.e., once each on beats 5 and 6 and again once each on beats 11 and 12.

SECOND MOVEMENT
(Tune *E Papa*)

The sequence of six movements shown below is done four times so that the movement occupies twenty-four beats.

Beat 1
Sticks held diagonally as shown in front of the body. Ends tapped on floor

Beat 2
Sticks brought up and tapped against the collar bone

Beat 3
As for beat 1

Beat 4
Sticks held by end and flipped over in a circular motion so that the sticks are caught by the opposite end

Beat 5
Sticks flipped again

Beat 6
Sticks held vertically and ends tapped on ground

THIRD MOVEMENT
(Tune *E Aue!*)

1. On the *first* beat of the bar, performers on each side of the leader tap their sticks on the ground (fig. 1, page 53). On the *second* beat, sticks are tapped together (fig. 2, page 53) and on the *third* beat each performer throws the stick in his inner hand inwards (as above) and simultaneously with the same hand catches the stick thrown to him.

2. Thus the leader (who has previously laid down his own sticks) finishes up with two sticks, as does everyone else, except the person on each end of the row is left with only one stick (see above).

3. In the second bar the movement is reversed and the sticks are thrown back again, so that everyone finishes up with two sticks, except the leader who has none.

4. This passing back and forth for every bar continues until the tune finishes.

FOURTH MOVEMENT
(Tune *Maku e!*)

| Front view | Side view | | Front view | Side view |

Maku e
Right stick is circled once clockwise around the left stick

ko-te o
Left stick is circled once anti-clockwise around the right stick

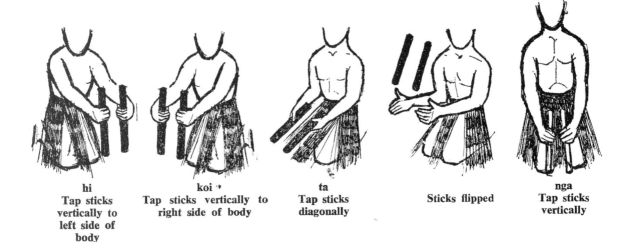

hi
Tap sticks vertically to left side of body

koi
Tap sticks vertically to right side of body

ta
Tap sticks diagonally

Sticks flipped

nga
Tap sticks vertically

FIFTH MOVEMENT
(Tune *Maku e*)

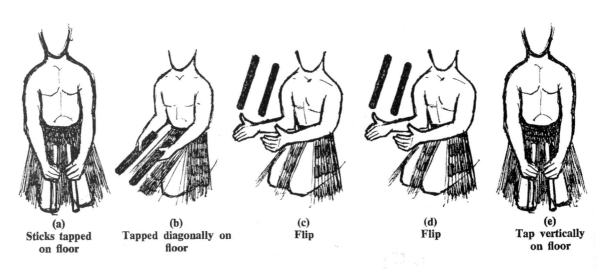

(a)
Sticks tapped on floor

(b)
Tapped diagonally on floor

(c)
Flip

(d)
Flip

(e)
Tap vertically on floor

Execution of Fifth Movement
This movement is staggered, with the performers divided into two groups, each of which works on different timings. Group 1 consists of the leader and the second, fourth, sixth, eighth, etc., performers from him on each side. Group two are the players in between the group 1 players in the row.

```
Words    Ma — ku  e  kau — te  o  hi......... — koi — ta........ — nga
Group 1  (a)      (b) (c) (d)     (e)              (a)   (b) (c)      (d)
Group 2                       (a) (b) (c) (d)      (e)
Words    Ma — ku  e  kau — te  o  hi......... — koi — ta........ — nga
Group 1  (e)                  (a) (b) (c) (d)      (e)
Group 2  (a)      (b) (c) (d)     (e)              (a)   (b) (c)   (d) (e)
```

CLOSING MOVEMENT

This movement returns the sticks so that they finish in a pile before the leader. It consists of the opening movement in reverse. First, all sticks in the player's inside hand are thrown from performer to performer until they reach the centre. Finally the sticks in the outside hand are thrown in.

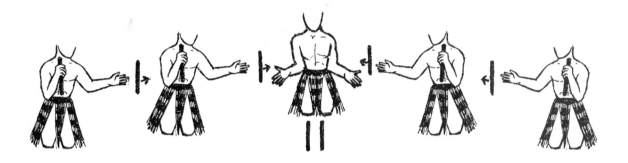

(a) First beat of bar: Tap sticks on floor (fig. 1, page 53)
(b) Second beat: Tap sticks together (fig. 2, page 53)
(c) Third beat: Throw sticks inwards (as illustrated above). Sticks in outside hands
                          are thrown in first.

61

8
MAORI STRING FIGURES (WHAI)

Origin and History

The making of string figures, or cat's cradle, as it is called in English, is known the world over and is a feature of Maori and other Polynesian cultures. The Maori version of the game was a popular pastime with young and old of both sexes. Usually the women were more proficient than men for, like all Maori games, string figures had their strictly utilitarian aspect. Proficiency at the game encouraged an agility with the fingers most necessary for the intricate arts of weaving and tukutuku work at which Maori women spent so much of their time. The game declined in popularity, and many of the old figures are not known today. Recently there has been a revival of interest however.

Myth claims that the game originated with Maui, the great culture hero of the Maori race, and it is sometimes called 'Maui,' but the more usual name is 'Whai' short for 'Te Whai Wawewawe a Maui'. The word 'whai' is sometimes used as a verb. For example, 'whaia ano' is a demand to execute again some particular movement of the game.

The Figures

In whai the figures are all given names and usually represent some object such as a fishing net, an incident in mythology, or some item of nature such as a star in the heavens. One traditional figure often mentioned is one which depicted the legendary ascent of Tawhaki and Karihi to the heavens. This was said to be a very large figure which when set up was nearly 270cm long. One person at each end made the design, while several others manipulated the centre of the pattern to show various stages in the progress of the legend.

This use of several people to form a complicated design is quite common, and sometimes it is necessary for participants to use their teeth and toes, as well as both hands, to hold the various loops. A three-person design is included in this chapter.

Learning Whai

A beginner should master one figure at a time, working slowly from the diagrams. If a figure does not come out, one must not be discouraged. Check step by step that the directions have been followed correctly, if necessary doing the figure while someone reads out the instructions. When some proficiency has been attained it is best to form the figures while singing some slow rhythmic tune as this helps movement at a constant speed. Later it is good practice to compete with a companion.

In days of old, two players would sit back to back and on a signal make a given figure. The first to finish would turn with a flourish and display it triumphantly to his opponent. Another variation, which emphasises technique rather than speed, is where the two competitors make their design and then turn around and compare the results.

Undoing a Figure

Unless a figure is taken apart correctly, many of them will leave the string in a very difficult tangle. Usually there are two straight lines along the top and bottom of any figure. Place the figure on a table, slip the fingers out and then draw these two straight strings apart and the figure will dissolve without any tangles.

The String

A medium gauge fishing cord makes the best string.

It should be at least 2m long and formed in a loop with the ends spliced or tightly sewn so as to make a smooth join.

1 — THE BASIC POSITION

The string is held on the hands in this way before any movement is begun.

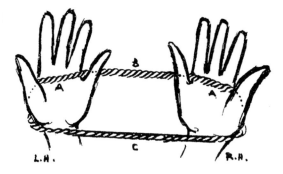

(a) The string across the palm (marked A) is the PALMAR STRING.

b) The string running between the little fingers (marked B) is the FAR LITTLE-FINGER STRING.

(c) The string running from thumb to thumb (marked C) is the NEAR THUMB STRING

2 — THE OPENING POSITION

The opening position is the beginning for most of the string figures. It is formed in four stages.

Stage 1

From the basic position with the RIGHT forefinger, pick up the left palmar string from below, allowing the loop to pass round the back of the RIGHT forefinger.

Stage 2

Pull the strings taut by parting the hands again. The string is round the back of the thumbs, across the palms and behind the little fingers.

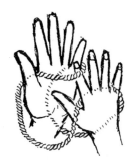

Stage 3

Pick up the RIGHT palmar string from below, using the left forefinger as shown.

Note carefully that the LEFT forefinger must be inserted at the base of the RIGHT forefinger, between the two strings round that finger.

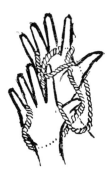

Stage 4

Bring the hands apart now to pull the string taut and we have the completed position as illustrated below. The following terms should be noted.

A is the *little-finger* loop (formed by the near and far little finger strings).

B is the *forefinger* loop (formed by the near and far forefinger strings).

C is the *thumb loop* (formed by the near and far thumb strings).

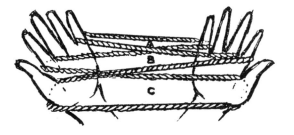

3 — THE TWO DIAMONDS FIGURE

This movement is completed in eight stages, beginning from the opening movement given in the bottom right-hand illustration on p.63.

Stage 1

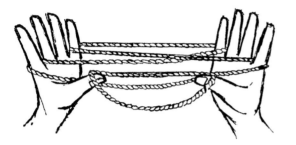

From the opening movement, slip the thumbs out of the thumb strings.

Stage 2

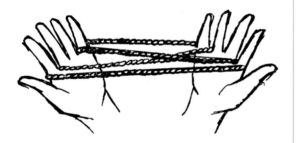

Pull the hands apart again so that the string is taut as above.

Stage 3

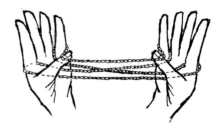

With the thumbs push down the *nearest* three strings. Then with the back of the thumbs pick up the far little finger string from below.

Stage 4

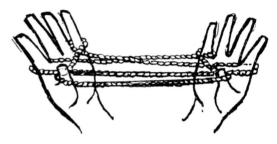

Still holding this far little-finger string on the *back* of the thumbs, pull it forward towards you until it becomes the string nearest the body.

Stage 5

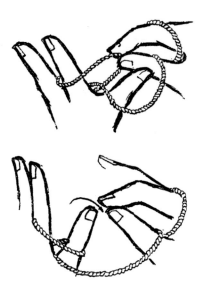

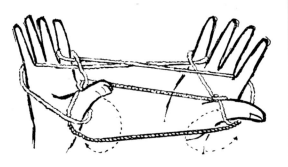

(a) With the opposite hand (or with your teeth) lift the near forefinger string of the LEFT hand over the top of the LEFT thumb.

(b) Then lift the same string of the RIGHT hand over the top of the RIGHT thumb.

Stage 6

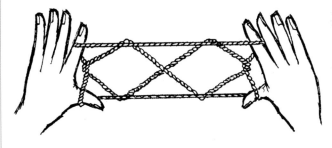

(a) Turn the thumbs down between the dotted string and the striped string.

(b) Then bring the thumb up again so that it is *in front* (i.e. nearest the body) of the striped string.

Stage 7

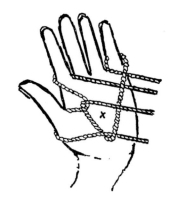

(a) Now turn the palms of the hand up so that a triangle appears at the base of each thumb.

(b) Put the tip of each forefinger through the triangle and keep it pressed on the base of the thumb at the point marked X.

(c) Then slip the little-finger strings.

Stage 8

Keeping the strings on the forefinger and thumb of each hand, turn the palms away and stretch wide.

4 — TOEMI FIGURE

This figure is one practised by the Te Aitanga-a-Mahaki tribe of Gisborne. A toemi is a type of net which has a mouth which can be drawn together like the mouth of a string bag. If the strings are held tight once the movement is complete, the toemi can be made to open and close by opening and closing the fingers and thumbs. Andersen records a little karakia which was sung to him by a Ngati Porou woman as she worked her figure, the fingers being spread wide on each accent.

Te *hope* tiwaiwaka

Te *hope* tiwaiwaka

The figure is completed in four stages, stage 1 being the basic position illustrated first in this chapter.

Stage 2

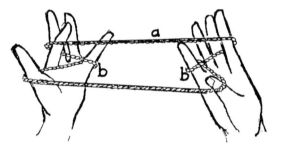

Place each forefinger under the far little-finger string and pull it taut as above.

Stage 3

(a) Pass the thumbs *over* the top of the near forefinger string (marked (a) in the stage 2 diagram) and *under* the far forefinger string (b).

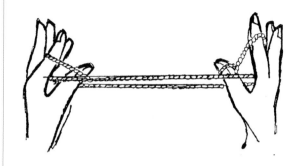

(b) Raise the thumbs now, taking the string on their backs.

Stage 4

(a) Turn the palms away from the body.

(b) Bend the wrists so that the hands bend inwards towards each other and the thumbs pass down between the near and far thumb strings.

(c) Now allow the near thumb string to pass over the tops of the thumbs. It will now be caught on the crossing of the string between forefinger and thumbs.

(d) Raise the hands to their original position.

(e) By opening and closing the thumb and forefinger, the 'mouth' of the 'net' will open.

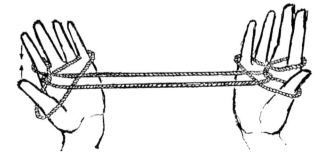

5 — MATAMATA KAHERU AND THE TRAP OF TAMA-TE-KAPUA

A kaheru is a spade, or any other implement for working the soil. Matamata kaheru is the flat of a spade, suggested by the triangular portions of the figure. In his book *Maori String Figures*, Anderson shows the Tuhoe method of making this figure, which is unknown to me. The Ngati Porou method which follows is characteristically simple.

Stage 1
Make the figure Toemi (fig. 4).

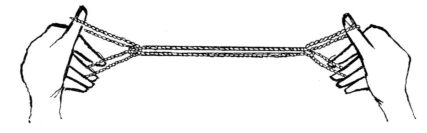

Stage 2
Slip the loops off the little fingers and complete the figure by drawing it taut as above.

Stage 3
The trap of Tama-te-Kapua is just a variation of the above figure carried out by three people.
(a) Two people take in each hand the thumb and index-finger loops of the matamata kaheru and spread them apart, drawing in to the centre the middle loop.
(b) The third person puts his finger into the loop to represent Tama-te-Kapua. The loop is drawn tight and Tama-te-Kapua is trapped by Uenuku, the Hawaiian chief whose enmity forced Tama and his people to flee to New Zealand in the *Arawa* canoe.

  Since Tama-te-Kapua is the father of the Arawa confederation of tribes, I presume that this is an Arawa figure (see p.63 of *Maori Action Songs* by the author and Reupena Ngata for more about Tama-te-Kapua).

6 — THE TAWHITI FIGURE

This figure is often done by Ngati Porou children. Tawhiti was a type of trap used for ensnaring the kiore, or native rat. I have sometimes heard the figure called tawhiti taratara, taratara being a short stick used in setting a tawhiti trap. A tawhiti kiore consisted of a number of upright sticks set in the ground joined by two horizontal vines inter-twined around the uprights in such a way as to form a number of diamond shapes. The figure is completed in nine stages from the opening position.

Stage 1

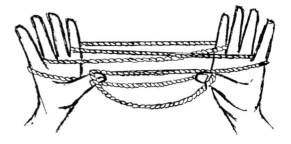

From the opening position slip the thumbs out of the thumb strings.

Stage 2

Turn the palms away from the body and pick up the far little-finger string from *below* with the back of each thumb and pull it up so that it is in front, nearest the body.

Stage 3

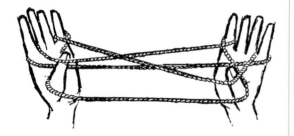

Turn the palms of the hand towards the body.
(a) with the base of the thumbs, press *down* on top of the near forefinger strings.
(b) Then with the backs of the thumbs pick up the far forefinger strings from below and pull up to the front.

Stage 4

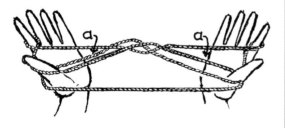

Slip the little fingers. There are now loops around the forefingers and thumbs.

Stage 5

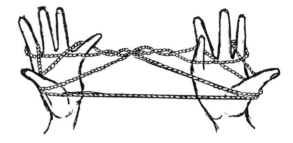

With the backs of the little-fingers, pick up the *far* thumb strings (marked (a) in stage 4) from below and pull back.

Stage 6

Slip the thumb strings. There should now be loops around the little-fingers and the forefingers and the strings have a crisscross effect.

Stage 7

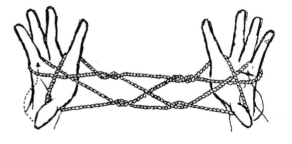

Carry the thumb up as is shown by the dotted arrows on the stage 6 diagram and pick up the near little-finger strings from below and pull them to the front as shown above.

Stage 8

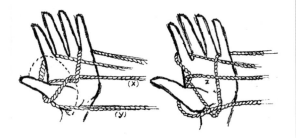

(a) Pick up the near forefinger string (marked (a) in diagram 4) and pull it over the thumb. The result will be as shown in the diagram above.

(b) Now turn each thumb down (as shown by the dotted line above in the left diagram) so that it passes between strings (x) and (y).

(c) Bring the thumbs up again *in front of* (y).

(d) Then turn the thumbs out again so that a triangle is formed at the base of thumbs (see right diagram).

Stage 9

(a) With the tip of each forefinger press down through the triangle on to point Z.

(b) Slip the little-finger strings.

(c) Turn the palm away and spread the thumbs and forefingers wide.

(d) To give a better effect, two people may grasp the thumb and forefinger loops of the completed figure in each hand and stretch them apart.

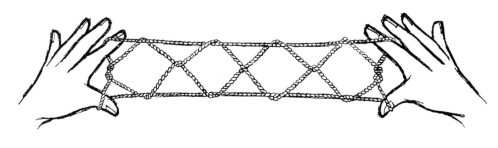

7 — TE WHARE KEHUA

The final result of this figure is very complicated to the uninitiated, but it is in fact very easy to execute and even to describe without diagrams. The whare kehua or, ghost house, is a Ngati Porou figure. It requires two persons and two strings. For the final three stages of the total of fourteen, a third person is required. The two persons with the string sit opposite one another. We shall call one A and the other B. The assistant is C.

Stage 1
Both players take up the opening position.

Stage 2
A passes his hands (with his string on them) completely through the loop formed by B's near and far forefinger string (the space marked B on the stage 4 diagram of the opening figure on p.63).

Stage 3
B slips his forefinger strings.

Stage 4
A pulls his hands back through the same loop as he first put them through in stage 2. As he does so he is careful to keep B's discarded forefinger strings on his wrist.

Stage 5
B passes his hands (with string attached) through the loop formed by A's near and far forefinger strings (loop B in stage 4 diagram of opening figure on p.63).

Stage 6

A slips his forefinger strings.

Stage 7

B pulls his hands out through A's loop. As he does so he takes care to keep A's forefinger strings on his (B's) wrist.

Stage 8

A turns his figure sideways so that the RIGHT hand is uppermost.

Stage 9

A passes his RIGHT hand over, and his LEFT hand under, B's figure, and then slips all fingers so that his string lies draped over B's figure.

Stage 10

A takes B's RIGHT thumb and RIGHT little-finger loops in his RIGHT and LEFT hands and B removes his LEFT hand completely from his figure.

Stage 11

C takes B's LEFT thumb and little-finger loops in his hands and B slips his hand completely out of the figure.

Stage 12

A and C now pull gently on their loops straight out

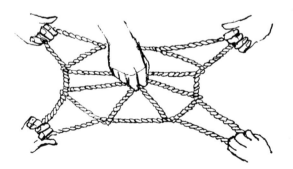

in a horizontal line so that the figure finally looks as it is shown in the diagram.

Stage 13

B places his thumb and little finger down through the loops marked X and hooks them up under the shaded string. He does the same through loop Y, using his forefinger and index finger.

Stage 14

A and C pull downwards on their loops and B pulls upward on his, and the result is the ghost house.

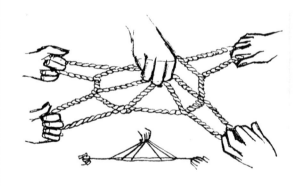

70

PART THREE

MAORI MUSIC AND MUSICAL DANCES

Introduction

This part of the book deals first with the subject of Maori music generally. Then follow chapters which deal in detail with the musical dances — action songs, powhiri and long and short poi. The shouted dances, haka taparahi and peruperu form Part 4.

Although there is some confusion on this, the term 'haka' means simply a dance of any type. Williams' Dictionary defines the word as 'dance' (noun and verb), and song accompanying a dance (noun and verb). As such, therefore, it includes both the musical dances which make up Part 3 of the book as well as those dances included in Part 4. Nowadays, however, the term has become more restricted in its connotation, and generally the term 'haka' refers to the vigorous posture dance, usually performed by men, in which the words are declaimed, not sung — in other words, the haka taparahi and peruperu featured in Part 4. To avoid confusion I have used 'haka' in its popular meaning as a generic term to embrace taparahi and peruperu. Action song, poi and powhiri are referred to by their correct specific names and NOT as haka.

Reupena Ngata and myself have already examined the modern action song in considerable detail in our book, *Maori Action Songs*, which gives numerous examples of action songs and includes words, translation, music and sketches of the actions, as well as full instruction on technique and performance. Therefore no attempt is made here to cover the action song in the detail which it would otherwise deserve, because undoubtedly it is the most popular and commonly performed aspect of Maori culture today. The chapter on action song in *Maori Games and Haka* is included merely for the sake of completeness and to serve as an introduction to an art form which has already merited a book to itself.

9

MAORI MUSIC AND MUSICAL INSTRUMENTS

Whenever the emotions of the Maori are aroused, they are likely to express themselves in song or chant. Few social gatherings take place without featuring music of some sort. When Sir Apirana Ngata farewelled Sir Peter Buck in the presence of distinguished guests in the Auckland Town Hall in 1947, he concluded his speech by intoning a chant. For the principal speaker suddenly to burst into song at a European gathering of a similar nature would be unthinkable. To a Maori the use of chant or song to express deep feeling is commonplace and appropriate.

Development of Maori Music

The development of Maori music is naturally a mirror of the recent evolution of the race. Before the European came, the music was primitive in quality and devoid of harmony and form as we know it today. With the coming of the Europeans, their musical idioms and styles were enthusiastically adopted at the expense of what had gone before. At first it was the hymn tunes which found favour and were adapted to other purposes. One poi tune still popular today is actually the music of a well known revivalist hymn. Then Maori songsters turned to the popular song with enthusiasm and not only borrowed current tunes but wrote new ones in the same idiom but to Maori words. The strong rhythm of the old music thus combined with the lilting melody of the new. In recent years, there has been a realisation that the past must not be discarded, and gradually the traditional material has returned

to favour. Thus we have modern chants and waiata of the flavour of 'Ka ru' and many others. These songs are infused with the harmonies of the new music and have a more modern form. At the same time they are reminiscent of, and owe much to, old chant and waiata. Now also there is a move away from adopting the Pakeha style in its entirety and instead it is being adapted to fit the Maori musical and emotional needs.

Pre-European Music

The songs of olden times can be divided into a number of types, depending on the reason for their composition. The main classes are lullabies (popo, oriori), laments (waiata tangi), abusive songs (patere), songs of defiance (kaioraora), love songs (waiata whaiaipo), ditties (ruri), prophetic songs (mata), chants (ngeri), songs sung on ceremonial occasions (tau), songs of victory (pioi and pihe), boat songs (hautu waka), work songs (tewha), tattooing songs (whakawai), and ritualistic chants (karakia). Nothing was too insignificant to serve as the theme of a song and the trivia of day-to-day happenings as well as the most momentous tribal events were commemorated in songs which often endured long after the occasion of their composition was forgotten.

The old music was lengthy, flowing and chant-like, with little tonal variation. It progressed in gradations of such minuteness that they are not readily apparent to the European ear. The requirement of rhythm transcended all else.

Rhyme was quite unknown, and certainly not sought after. Indeed, the way in which the music was sung would have submerged any rhyming effect. As can be expected, the translation of much of the ancient material presents great difficulty, for meaning was often subordinated to sound and rhythm and there are many obscure references to long forgotten happenings, people and legends.

With the karakia or religious invocations, great importance was attached to correct enunciation and delivery of the words. Not only would an incorrectly chanted karakia be ineffective but the perpetrator of the outrage was in great danger of incurring the wrath of the gods. Two persons, or even a team, were needed for the longer karakia, so that before the first person's breath failed the other took up the chant in order that it might continue without a break.

Of ancient Maori music, Captain Cook said: 'They sang a song with a degree of taste that surprised us, the tune was solemn and slow like those of our psalms, containing many tones and semitones.' Dr Savage, writing in 1807, said: 'The tone of voice of the natives is, in a considerable degree, melodious. Here every man is his own musician and the instrument he plays upon, being conveniently portable, he is never at a loss for the means of entertainment.'

Modern Music

With the advent of the nineteenth century and the coming of the European, Maori music, in common with the music of all cultures at the time, underwent a profound change. When Maori take straight European tunes, with few exceptions the music undergoes a subtle change. The rhythm and style in which they are sung are Maori, not European. In any case the Maori regards the tune as principally a vehicle for the words. It is the words and the emotion they convey which are important. European musical notation is often not quite adequate to express music the way a typical Maori group will sing it. Songs are sung in long flowing phrases and punctuated where desired. Syncopation is frequent and mischievous and the occasional extra beat is put in here and there just to make things interesting. Pauses are lengthened or shortened as fancy dictates.

Maori music is a reflection of the changing life of Maori and of the sharing of Pakeha and Maori cultures. Like a language, music must develop and progress. Furthermore, in addition to much music of the popular variety there is also some serious Maori music being written today which represents a skilful blending of old and new.

ANCIENT MAORI MUSICAL INSTRUMENTS

The Maori had a number of musical instruments as well as many devices which are noise-making toys rather than instruments. Musical instruments can be broadly grouped into four classes – drums, gongs, wind instruments and stringed instruments. The Maori did not have a drum. In their dances the rhythmic stamping of feet provided the beat as well as any drum. There were various types of war gongs. Some were of hollowed logs or trees, others were solid with a slot, and the sound was made through rattling a stick from side-to-side of the slot. The true pahu, however, seems to have been a thick plank with a groove cut down the length and suspended by ropes. Early writers speak of gongs, which varied from 2m to 4m long and gave off sounds which could be heard up to 30km away! Another percussion instrument was the tokere, or castanets, made from shell.

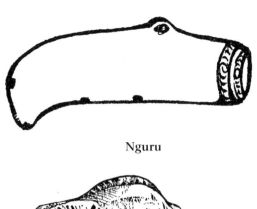

Nguru

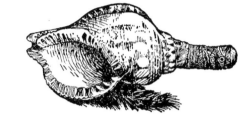

Shell and wooden trumpets

Koauau

The most usual instruments were wind-blown. There were a number of types of flute, the groups being porutu made from wood with one end closed, whio made from wood and played by blowing across the upper end, koauau made from wood or bone and played either by the nose or the lips blowing across the open upper end, and finally the nguru or whistle flute, which was of wood, stone or whale ivory. The nguru was short and slightly curved and seems to have been played by blowing across the open end, although there is some doubt about this.

The trumpets, or pu were made from flax, shell, wood or calabash. There was also a bull-roarer, or purerehua, which was whirled around in the air on the end of a string. It made a whirring noise and featured in rain-making ceremonies. The only evidence that the Maori had a stringed instrument rests on the statement of an early visitor, Canon Stack, who claims to have seen an instrument called ku. He described it as shaped like a bow; 25cm long, made out of hardwood. The single string was made from flax and the sound came from tapping the string with a rod. Buck states that in his opinion it was probably a child's toy, rather than a string instrument.

10

THE POWHIRI (DANCE OF WELCOME)

Social Significance

To the Maori, hospitality is and always has been a virtue to be prized above most others. Even today the full ceremony of welcome is enacted on auspicious occasions before distinguished guests. In its form it differs little from that of days long gone. Although there are differences between tribes, the ingredients of the ceremony are similar everywhere. Protocol must be punctiliously observed on such occasions.

The Ancient Maori Welcome

There was no such thing as an unexpected call, unless one came as the enemy. (Even then, the Maori was a chivalrous opponent and often liked to give his enemy every chance in order to make a fight worthwhile.) The visitors would approach a village with their leaders in front. Warned by the kaiwhakaara (watchman), high in his puhara or watchtower, the inhabitants of the pa would make ready. If they were unsure of their visitors they would stay within the confines of the pa. If the visit had been expected and it was already known that the visitors came in peace, the home people would rush from the pa, naked as if going into battle and waving their clothing. They would always draw up well short of the advancing group.

Then began the wero (sometimes called taki) or ceremony of challenge. The first challenger would come forward. His task was to identify the approaching group, and he carried in his hand the rakau whakaara or challenging spear. When he was close enough to identify the visitors he would lay the spear either across their path, which signified peace, or pointing at them, which denoted that the home people regarded their visitors as hostile. If this latter was the case, the spear was sometimes thrown instead of being placed down, but usually it would be placed in the peaceful position in order to deceive the group into thinking that they would be peacefully received. The visitors would take no notice of the rakau whakaara but would continue their measured, silent tread forward.

Next came a second challenger with the rakau whakaoho, the alerting or protecting spear. His mission was to get more specific information about the strength and fighting potentialities of the group. He would place or cast his spear in the same way as the first challenger and return to the pa. Finally it was the turn of the principal challenger. This third warrior would come forward with the rakau whakawaha, or all-clear, spear. After laying it down he would perform an intricate drill with his his taiaha, or long club, with much grimacing and little yelping cries, finishing in an over and forward beckoning movement of the weapon. If the home group were convinced of the visitors hostility, the culmination of the third challenge would be the challenger slapping his thigh, then turning and speeding back to the safety of the palisade, pursued by the fastest runner from the visitors. If the challenger was caught there would be a duel. If the challenger won the war might be replaced by a treaty of peace.

Sometimes this pursuing of the challenger would take place even when the mission was peaceful. It was a very bad omen for the hosts if their challenger was caught before he had gained the security of the home ranks. Finally, ranged up before their hosts, the visitors would drop down onto one knee, watching the home people, who were similarly down on one knee. Suddenly, as one man, the hosts would jump to their feet and perform a peruperu, or war dance with weapons, to which the visitors were expected to reply. These peruperu after the wero showed the visitors that not only were the home people always alert and ready for battle, but that they considered their visitors worthy of their efforts had they in fact been hostile.

If the leaders of the visitors were sufficiently important they were not expected to use the normal entrance to the pa. Instead a section of the palisading would be torn down to allow them to enter followed by their people. After the peruperu the men gave way to the women. The high, shrill karanga or call of welcome from a tribal spokeswoman or spokesman would be the signal to move forward to the marae, which was the courtyard before the principal building of the village, usually the whare runanga or public meeting house. There the womenfolk would stand beckoning their guests with twigs of greenery in time to the rhythmic chant of the powhiri or dance of welcome.

When the powhiri was finished, the men would come through the ranks of the women or use the tama-tane approach (see chapter on concert entrances) and perform another dance before the visitors. This was often a haka taparahi, or dance without weapons, and in this capacity it was, unlike the peruperu performed earlier, not an indication of vigilance but an assertion of the dominion of the tribe over the village and its surrounds.

As has been said, the order of events varies to some extent according to circumstances and tribe. At this stage might come the tangi. This was the ritual weeping as a mark of respect to those who had died and could not be present on this occasion.

Te roimata i heke
Te hupe i whiua ki te marae
Ka ea aitua!
The tears which fall
The mucus which is cast on the marae
Avenge death!

When the guests finally reached the principal building, speechmaking or whaikorero would take place. This could last for many hours. Graceful compliments were made and replied to. There was much polished oratory, containing metaphor and allusion to mythology and chants and laments. Each host speaker finished with the standard phrase of greeting, 'Haere mai! Haere mai! Haere mai!' (Welcome, thrice welcome). Even today the order of speechmaking differs from tribe to tribe. Among the Aotea tribes of the West Coast at tangi welcomes, the visitors will speak first, followed by the tangata whenua or local people. The opposite applies among Ngati Raukawa and Ngati Porou. Among Waikato each host speaker is replied to by a visiting speaker.

Lastly came hongi or the nose-pressing ceremony. The home people would form a line and the visitors would pass down the line giving each person the traditional hongi – the pressing (not rubbing) of noses. Sometimes this part of the ceremony would take place directly after the powhiri. Once protocol was satisfied and ceremony was concluded, the marae was said to be noa or free from tapu, and the visitors would sit down to the finest feast their hosts could provide.

The Maori Welcome of Today
Now the old courtesies have been adapted to the needs of modern times. The distinguished guest (or guests) is challenged (usually) by a single warrior bearing a short, sometimes carved, rod in lieu of the challenge spear. Laying down the rod on the

ground before the visitor, the challenger goes through the intricate mincing movements of the wero, brandishing his taiaha, but always taking care to ensure that the tongue of the weapon does not point directly at the visitor. When the warrior retires, the ancient ceremony of chasing is symbolised by the visitor picking up the rod and moving forward to the marae, where the women still stand waving their green leaves and performing the powhiri.

Speeches are much shorter and will sometimes be bilingual, in English after the Maori. Nevertheless the Maori portion follows traditional custom by making reference first to the meeting house before which the ceremony is being enacted, then to the marae, then to the dead and finally to the living. Speeches are interspersed with musical and other items which the Maori call the kinaki, or relish. There is unlikely to be a hongi unless the visitors are Maori, and then it will probably be accompanied by that Pakeha innovation, the handshake. However, the Maori handshake is not the firm clasp which Europeans often use as a measure of warmth of welcome, but rather a light joining together of the hands.

The Powhiri

This chapter is a brief examination of the powhiri, or dance of welcome. As the powhiri, unlike other dances, does not exist in isolation but is an integral part of complicated ceremony and protocol, some space has, as a preliminary, been devoted to examining it within the context of the whole ceremony of welcome to visitors. There is nothing standardised about the powhiri, except the waving of the green branches by the women. This has possibly stemmed from the ancient custom mentioned previously of the welcomers waving their clothing at guests. On certain occasions clusters of greenery were worn as garments. Apart from this convention, any song or dance which expresses the sentiment of welcome is a powhiri. Sometimes it is chanted, but often today European idiom is used.

POWHIRI – *KA TANUKU*

The first part of the powhiri which follows is an adaptation of an old haka. The powiri was first performed for a great welcome to the men of C (Ngaati Porou) Company of the Maori Battalion at Poho-o-Rawiri marae, Gisborne, at the end of the Second World War. It has been frequently performed since then at many gatherings with other names of local significance substituted for Hikurangi. It is particularly suitable as a patere before a tangi. It may be thought strange that a welcome song has such sombre words, but it is common Maori custom to refer to those who cannot be present when welcoming those who are.

Kaea:	Ka tanuku!	'Tis shrouded!
Katoa:	E!	E!
Kaea:	Ka tanuku!	'Tis covered!
Katoa:	E!	E!
	Ka tanuku koa	'Tis veiled!
	Te tihi o Hikurangi	The summit of Hikurangi
	Ka tanuku! A! Ha! Ha! Aue!	Is veiled in sorrow!
	E kapo ki te whetu	Let me seize the evening star
	E kapo ki te marama	Let me ensnare the moon
	E kapo ki te ata	Let me enchain the soul
	O aku (taku) raukura	Of my loved ones
	Ka riro	Who have fallen …
Kaea:	Toia mai!	O ye who are welcomed, draw hither!
Katoa:	Te waka!	Like the canoe!
Kaea:	Ki te urunga!	To its resting place!
Katoa:	Te waka!	The canoe!
Kaea	Ki te moenga!	To its abiding place!
Katoa:	Te waka!	The canoe!
Kaea:	Ke te takotoranga i takoto ai!	To the place where it is to lie!
Katoa:	Te waka!	The canoe!

The second half of the powhiri is the well known canoe-hauling chant or ngeri, *Toia Mai*, in which the visitors coming onto the marae are likened to the canoe coming to its resting place.

Rhythm

Ka tanu (beat) *ku E!* (repeat)

Ka tanu (beat) ku koa

Te tihi *o* Hikura*ngi*

Ka tanu (beat) ku *A* ha *ha* Aue!

E kapo *ki* te whe*tu*

E kapo *ki* te ma*rama*

E kapo *ki* te ata (beat)

O aku *rau*kura

ka riro

Toia *mai! Te* waka

Ki te uru*nga! Te* waka

Ki te moenga! Te* waka

Ki te ta*kotoranga i takoto ai te* wa... *ka*

Note that when the actions begin, the deep foot action common to tunes in waltz-time is used (see next frame).

Leader calls "Ruia" and the sprigs are waved across the front of the body once to each beat of the rhythm until . . .

. . . on "E kapo" (8th line) the action changes to that shown above one action on each beat. This action continues until . . .

From . . . . .To

. . . on "ka riro" the two actions above are carried out three times.

This action commences on "Toia mai" and continues until the end of the powhiri. The sprig in the right hand is carried in towards the mouth and out again to the right, as shown on successive beats. Care must be taken not to move the greenery so as to obscure the face.

POWHIRI — *HAERE MAI E HOA MA*

This is a modernised version of a very old chant.

Haere mai e hoa ma!	Welcome, ye many friends!
Nga iwi o te motu,	And tribes throughout the land,
Ki runga o tenei marae.	To this, our marae.
Tenei te powhiri atu	Listen to the welcome song
A te iwi. Haere mai!	Of the people! Welcome!
A (place name) haere mai!	Of (place name), welcome!
Tahi, rua, toru, wha.	One, two, three, four.
Haere mai te manuhiri,	Welcome to our guests,
Haere mai, haere mai!	Thrice welcome!
Haere mai te manuhiri,	Welcome to our many guests,
No runga te manuhiri,	From the south ye have come
No raro te manuhiri,	From the north ye have come,
No te ti, no te ta, hei ha!	From hither, from thither,
E haere mai!	Welcome!

twice

Haere mai e hoa ma

twice

Nga iwi o te motu

Ki runga o tenei marae.

Tenei te powhiri atu,

A te iwi   Haere mai

A Poneke, haere mai!

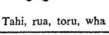

Tahi, rua, toru, wha

Turn to face left

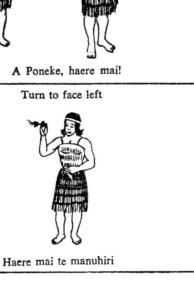

Haere mai te manuhiri

Haere mai   Haere mai

twice

Haere mai te manuhiri.

No runga te manuhiri

No raro te manuhiri

No te ti   No te ta

Hei ha!   E haere mai

11

THE POI DANCE (HAKA POI)

General

Few if any of the arts of the Maori appeal more than the graceful movements of the poi. The haka taparahi and the action song have their equivalent elsewhere in Polynesia but the poi is distinctive to New Zealand. There is a consummate artistry about a well executed poi dance which never fails to delight the onlooker. The late Alfred Hill captured the spirit when he wrote in his famous song *Waiata Poi*, 'watch her supple wrist and the poi twirl and twist, hear the gentle tapping against the raupo wrapping of this fascinating thing.'

There are two types of poi dance – that using the long poi and that using the more familiar short poi. It is said that in the days of old, the long poi was one of the arts taught only to women of high rank. Its technique was jealously guarded and not passed on to the lower classes, who in the end, devised the short poi and perfected the art of twirling it for their own amusement and as a counter attraction to the dance done by their betters.

The Poi

The poi were works of art in themselves. The dressed fibre of the flax plant was woven into a fine textured material and this covered an inner filling made from the pappus of the bulrush. The cover was often adorned with taniko designs in geometric shapes, formed by weaving dyed fibres into the fabric. Long white dog hair or feathers were usually attached to the collar of the ball. These poi with the dog hair were called poi awe, wheras the ordinary poi was poi kokau.

For practical purposes it is best to make a poi which will stand considerable use. The usual method is to roll paper into a ball about 10cm in diameter and cover this with unbleached calico or muslin. Tie or stitch the material firmly around the collar and attach the string. The string should be thick cord, with a reasonably sized knot at the far end to facilitate holding. The string for short poi is about 22cm long and that of the long poi, the length of the user's arm.

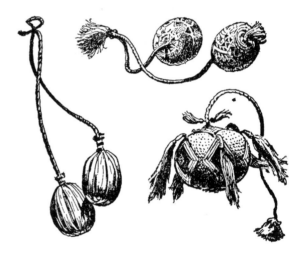

The Dance

The poi was accompanied by a rhythmic chant or the men shouting a haka. These are still used, but it is more common nowadays for a European-type tune in two-four, three-four, or four-four time to be used. Several examples are given in this chapter. Generally the dance group will stand in rows, as for an action song, but considerably more space must be left between individuals. Some poi, such as the famous waka or canoe poi, are performed kneeling or sitting.

A dance consists of a number of different figures. Each of these figures is performed for the length of one verse of the song (normally eight bars) and the song is sung as many times as is necessary to carry out all the figures of the particular dance. Usually the last line is repeated and during this, the leader (who also controls the rhythm of the dance) will do the next action to show the group what is to follow.

There are, of course, as many figures as human ingenuity can devise, and those that follow are just a few. They are what is generally regarded as being the 'basic' figures. They can be performed in any order to any suitable tune and individuals can make up their own dances accordingly.

Handling the Ball

Performers begin the dance with the backs of the fingers resting lightly on the hips. The poi cord is held between the thumb and the first finger, with the end knot in the palm of the hand and the ball hanging free. The patting of the poi in movements with the single poi is done with the fingers and, in the case of the short poi, the back of the hand. It is a light tap only, designed to arrest the poi ball and change its direction of swing.

The Leg Movement

The leg movement for the dance is similar to that of the action song, which is fully dealt with in the chapter relating to teaching technique. Some tribes prefer the foot action where the balls of both feet are kept on the ground and the timing marked by a raising and lowering of the heels.

Learning the Poi

With the short poi nothing further should be attempted until the poi twirl is thoroughly mastered. In the long poi, the essential preliminary is a perfecting of the simple swinging of the poi in circular movements. It is best to try for equal facility in each movement with both hands before progressing. This avoids the pitfall of becoming adept at using one hand and then experiencing difficulty in coordinating movements with two hands in the double poi, or becoming more adept at using one hand than the other, which produces an uneven figure. As with all other Maori dances, practise before the mirror is recommended.

SOME POI SONGS

Following are several well-known poi songs ranging from the very simple *Haere mai e Hine Ma* (Come, maidens) to the complex, syncopated *Waikato*. There are, of course, dozens of so-called poi songs but few, if any, have been specifically written for poi, and any song in four-four or waltz time will do admirably.

HAERE MAI E HINE MA or HOEA RA
TE WAKA NEI

This famous and well-loved song was composed in part by the late Sir Apirana Ngata who also translated it into English. It was used first as part of the appeal to recruit men for the Maori contingent in the First World War and also to raise money for the Maori Soldiers Fund. Later it was sung at the great hui at Gisborne when the men were welcomed back from overseas.

1 Haere mai e hine ma
  Me nga taonga o te wa
  He reo karanga i katoa
  Haere mai ki a au

  Chorus
  Hoea ra te waka nei
  Hoea hoea ki te pai
  Ma te poi e karawhiu
  E rahui i te pai

2 Me pehea ra e taea ai
  Te aroha e pehi kino nei
  Mo te tau i pamamao
  Haere mai ki a au

  Chorus
  Hoea ra te waka nei, etc.

3 Koia ra e hine ma
  Koha kore noa te pai
  Haere mai te atawhai
  Ka rahui i te pai

4 Na te ngakau tangi ra
  Ko te tiwaiwaka nei
  Te poi ra hoea atu nei
  Hei tohu i te pai

Come maidens come to me
With your gift of melody
Crying near and far to all
Come where duty calls

Then together we will draw
This canoe until the end
To the goal the world desires
Peace and joy for all

Would you still the longing heart
Ease the pain that gnaws within
For the dear ones far away
Gone where duty calls

Cleared by war of all its dross
Love is gleaming strong and bright
In our hearts we vow to serve
Where our duty calls

Small may be this our canoe
Floating in a sea of tears
Tribute to the brave who fell
Where their duty called

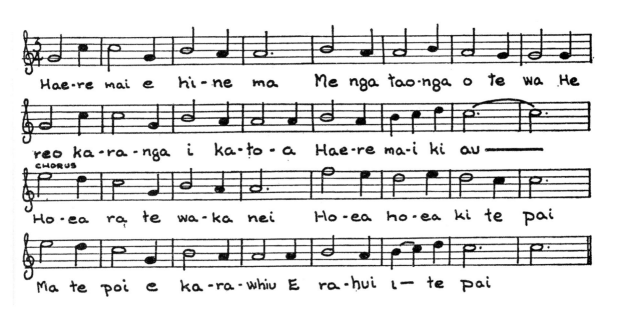

HE PURU TAITAMA and TOIA MAI TE WAKA

Next is a bracket of two well-known songs: *He Puru Taitama* by that most prolific and well loved composer of Maori songs, the late Kingi Tahiwi, and *Toia mai te Waka*. Quite often during a poi item the performers will switch without pause from one song to another.

He puru taitama e   I am a young playboy
He puru taitama hoki   Very much a playboy
He puru taitama   A playboy from Otaki
He puru n' Otaki   Full of the joys of life
He puru tukituki e

Toia mai te waka e te iwi e   Row the canoe ye people
Nei te ara pai kumea mai   With a will, along the path of duty
Kaua ra e pehi kino te purei   Do not let misfortune oppress you
To koutou hoa ra i enei takiwa   We are all friends together

WAIKATO

This song, as the title suggests, is about the Waikato tribes. The words following are in praise of Koroki, the leader of the Maori King Movement, whose marae is at Turangawaewae, Ngaruawahia. These words are slightly altered from the original. The tune is Rarotongan. Of all the tribes, those of Waikato, incensed by the mass confiscation of land inflicted on them as retribution supposedly for their part in the wars of the last century, refused to cooperate with the government over the matter of recruiting Maori in the First World War. As a result, the conscription principle embodied in the Military Service Act 1916 was, by consent of the other tribes, extended in 1917 to include Maori. Waikato still held out, however, and in order to assert the law, the government took a number of young Waikato men compulsorily into camp at Narrow Neck. One of these was young Te Rau-angaanga, brother of Rata Mahuta, the then King. As a gesture of solidarity towards Waikato in their time of trouble, some supporters, who were part Rarotongan, composed this song in its original form.

The tune is basically simple but the words are complicated and some facility is necessary to fit them to the tune.

E noho Koroki te Hiiri o Waikato
E huri to kanohi ki te Hauauru
Nga hau e ngunguru i waho o Te Akau
Aui, hai aue!

Reign oh Koroki, monarch of Waikato
Turn your face to the West
O winds that thunder from Te Akau

To pikitaanga ko runga o te rangi
To heketanga ko Karioi maunga
To hoenga waka i Whaingaroa
Aui, hai aue!

Climb to the very skies
Descend even to Mount Karioi
Paddle your canoe to Whaingaroa

Takahia atu ra te moana i Aotea
Kia whatiwhati koe i te pua o te miro
Te tihi o Moerangi, te puke okiokinga
Aue! Hai aue!

You have trod the coastline of Aotea
To pluck the plumes of the miro
On the crest of Moerangi, the resting place

Tairi te aroha a ha ha
Toro mai o ringa me aroha taua
Aui e! Aui e! Aui hai aue!

Hold fast to your love
Extend to me the hand of affection

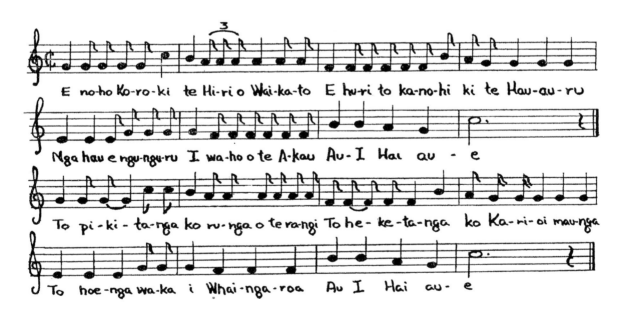

87

SOME POI FIGURES

DOUBLE LONG POI

The double long poi is given first because it is more simple to learn, strangely enough, than the single long poi. In the single poi there are the lightning changes of the poi from hand to hand, and much greater dexterity is called for. The double poi, however, calls for coordination of hand and eye in those movements where the manipulation of the poi in the left hand differs from that in the right, and helps the novice to get the feel of the poi and the rhythm of the dance.

1 — FORWARD SWING (Chorus movement)

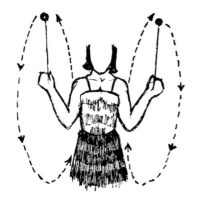

Most poi dances begin with an introductory chorus to establish rhythm and speed and often finish with the same chorus. The poi are swung as shown above during the singing of these choruses. Keep the elbows as close to the sides as possible and use the wrists to swing the poi.

2 — THE CROSSED ARMS SWING

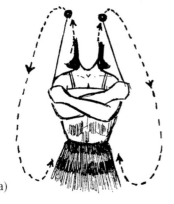

(a)

(1) Swing the poi once forward vertically as shown in the chorus movement.
(2) Cross the arms as shown in diagram (a) with the left forearm outside the right, and complete another swing forward.
(3) Uncross the arms and swing the poi forward again as shown in the chorus movement.

(b)

(4) Cross the arms below the waist as in diagram (b) and swing the poi behind the body so that they slap the buttocks.

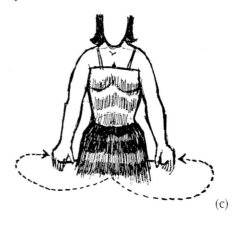

(c)

(5) Uncross the hands as shown in diagram (c) and again swing the poi behind the body, but this time the left poi goes around the left side of the body

and the right poi around the right side. Keep the hands in front of the body during the movement and avoid carrying them to the rear.

(6) Swing the poi forward, and then reverse the direction of swing as the hands are brought up to waist level so that the movement finishes with a forward swing as shown in the chorus movement.

3 — THE OVERHEAD UNDERWAIST SWING

(d)

(1) Swing the RIGHT poi above the head twice, ant-clockwise (diagram d).

(e)

(2) At the same time, swing the LEFT poi around the right side of the body (diagram d) so that it slaps the left buttock once, and then around the left side of the body (diagram e). Make sure that the left hand remains in front of the body.

(f)

(3) Reverse the movement and carry out the above again, but swing the LEFT poi above the head and the RIGHT poi below waist level, first to the left side and then to the right (diagram f).

4 — THE FORWARD AND BACKWARD SWING

(g)

(1) Holding the hands as shown in diagram (g) swing both poi across the body, anti-clockwise.

89

(h)

(2) Manipulating the wrist so that the poi inscribes a figure of eight, lift the hands so that they are above the shoulder as shown in diagram (h).

(3) The poi circle once behind the body (diagram h).

(4) Bring the hands down and begin the movement again from the start.

5—THE UNDERARM PAT

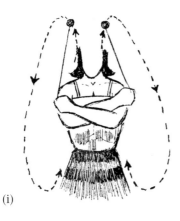

(i)

(j)

(k)

(l)

(1) Cross the arms as in diagram (i) and swing the poi once forward.

(2) Uncross the arms as in diagram (j) and complete another circle.

(3) Drop the hands and swing the poi up under the armpit, as shown in (k), so that they hit the shoulder-blades, and then swing them forward again.

(4) Swing the poi up and over the shoulder so that they curl over behind the back and under the armpit, where they are slapped back by the open palm (l).

(5) Cross the arms and repeat the movement.

6 — THE KNECK AND WAIST SWING

This movement follows on after a chorus.

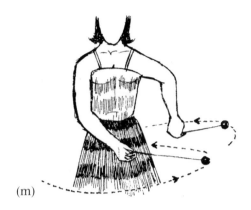

(m)

(1) Swing the poi around the left hip so that they slap against the buttock (diagram m).

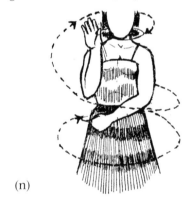

(n)

(2) Swing the LEFT poi around the RIGHT hip (diagram n).

(3) Simultaneously, swing the RIGHT poi around the neck (diagram n) and pat it back with the palm of the RIGHT hand.

(4) As the RIGHT poi swings back, lower the RIGHT hand and swing the poi around the LEFT hip (diagram o).

(o)

(5) Simultaneously, swing the LEFT poi around the neck, and then pat it back with the palm of the LEFT hand (diagram o).

7 — SINGLE HAND MOVEMENT

(p)

(1) Swing both poi as shown in diagram (p). The RIGHT poi swings anti clockwise, the LEFT swings clockwise.

(2) This should be continued until the poi are swung freely and easily.

(3) Then slowly bring the hands together until the RIGHT hand comes over the top of the LEFT. Now move the hands up and down to keep the poi swinging.

(4) Now transfer the cord end of the bottom poi to between the little and third fingers of the right hand.

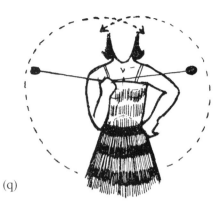

(q)

(5) Continue to swing the poi in opposite directions by moving the RIGHT hand up and down (diagram q).

(6) Once the above is completely mastered, the poi can be lifted over to swing behind the body.

THE SINGLE LONG POI

1 — THE FIGURE OF EIGHT MOVEMENT

(a)

The poi is swung through a figure of eight arc as illustrated, beginning with a circle to the left, and then one to the right. The elbow should stay as close to the body as possible, the impetus for the swing coming from the wrist rather than from an arm action.

2 — THE FORWARD PAT

(b)

(1) For the start of this movement, the RIGHT arm is at waist level, as shown, with the palm away from the body.

(2) Hold the end of the string in the palm of the RIGHT hand with the thumb. The string comes up the back of the fingers of the RIGHT hand and is held in the LEFT hand between thumb and forefinger. Thus the poi hangs down in front of the RIGHT hand.

(3) Now the poi is patted forward first by the fingers of the RIGHT hand. As the poi swings forward, the end of the string is allowed to slide up until caught in the LEFT hand. At the same moment the level of the hands is reversed, the LEFT hand coming down with the palm turned away from the body ready to pat the poi, the RIGHT hand coming up under the cord. The movement is really easier to do than it is to describe.

3 — THE SIDEWAYS PAT

(c)

(1) Hold the poi as shown in diagram (c).

(e)

(3) At the same time, release the cord end so that it slides through to be caught by the fingers of the RIGHT hand (diagram e).

(d)

(2) Pat the poi with the LEFT hand so that it swings to the RIGHT, up and over (diagram d).

(f)

Bring the LEFT hand over so that the poi falls across it (diagram f). Bring the RIGHT hand down into position to tap the poi back so that it swings in the opposite direction and the movement is repeated (diagram f).

4 — THE FORWARD AND SIDEWAYS PAT

(1) Hold the poi as in diagram (g) with end of cord in RIGHT hand.

(2) Pat the poi forward with the RIGHT hand, holding the string firmly in the LEFT hand between forefinger and thumb.

(3) A turning movement of the LEFT hand flicks the poi so that it swings over in a circle outside the

left arm and then swings down and in again from the left.

(4) As the poi swings down it is hit back again by the RIGHT hand (diagram h). At the same time, the end of the cord slips through to the LEFT hand, the RIGHT hand moves up so that the poi falls over it (diagram i) and the poi is tapped back in the opposite direction by the LEFT hand (diagram i).

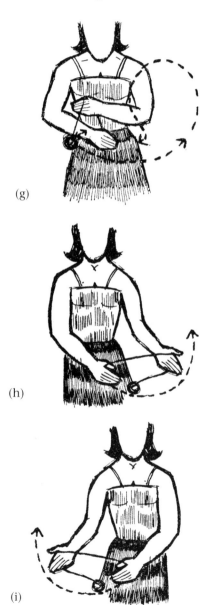

(g)

(h)

(i)

5 — THE UNDERARM PAT

(j)

(1) Perform the action shown in diagram (j) —the forward pat—twice.

(2) After the second pat the cord is held firmly in the LEFT hand.

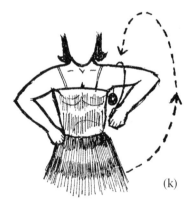

(k)

(3) The LEFT hand lifts the poi up and flicks it over the LEFT shoulder so that it connects with the LEFT hand under the armpit, as shown in diagram (k).

(4) The poi is patted back so that it swings back over the shoulder again.

(l)

(5) The poi is carried down to waist level by the LEFT hand and falls across the RIGHT hand, which is waiting to receive it (diagram l).

(6) At the same time the LEFT palm turns to the front to pat the poi back (diagram m) and the forward pat (diagram j) is repeated.

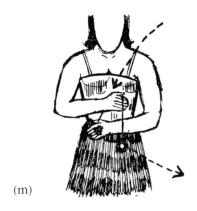

(m)

(7) Now the end of the cord is in the RIGHT hand and movements (3) and (4) are carried out, only this time over the right shoulder.

The movement continues to the end of the musical verse, with two forward pats taking place between each underarm pat.

THE SINGLE SHORT POI

Although opinions will differ, the short poi is generally regarded as being more difficult to master than the long poi. It demands a much greater dexterity and sense of timing. The beginner must first master the difficult art of twirling the poi before attempting any of the movements.

TWIRLING THE POI

(a)

(1) The poi is suspended as shown in diagram (a). For clarity the poi string is shown slightly longer than normal.

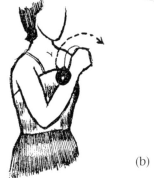

(b)

(2) With a quick wrist movement, the hand is flicked up and the poi follows in a circle until it smacks against the back of the hand, as is shown in diagram (b).

(3) The poi bounces off the back of the hand and as the ball swings down, the hand twists over from the wrist (a) so that the palm is facing up. Thus the poi describes a circle and comes up to hit the back of the hand from beneath.

(4) Bouncing off, the poi swings back to the starting position and the movement begins again.

1 — POROTITI (TWIRL)

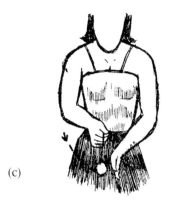

(c)

(1) The RIGHT hand twirls the poi to the RIGHT.
(2) While this is being done, the LEFT arm moves across slightly from the waist so that the poi beats gently against the hand (diagram c) on downward swing.

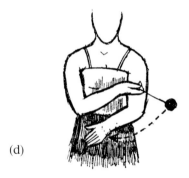

(d)

(3) The dancer then lifts her RIGHT hand again so that the poi lifts over and hits against the back of the LEFT hand.
The two movements alternate so that the poi hits the palm, then the back, palm, back, etc. each time marking the beat of the tune.

2 — PUPURI (HOLD)

(e)

(1) The LEFT hand holds the poi lightly (diagram e).

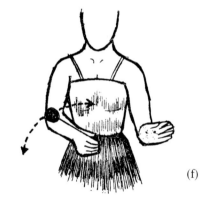

(f)

(2) Twirl the poi once to the RIGHT (f).
(3) Catch the poi in the LEFT hand (e).
This movement should take two beats. The poi is held momentarily in the LEFT hand until the second beat is completed, and then the whole movement is repeated on the third and fourth beats of the bar.

3 — PEKE (SHOULDER)

(g)

(1) Begin with the poi over the RIGHT shoulder (diagram g).

(h)

(2) Beats 1 and 2: Bring the poi down to the LEFT hand (diagram h).

(i)

(3) Beats 3 and 4: Bring the poi back to the RIGHT shoulder (diagram I).

4 — HOPUHOPU (CATCH)

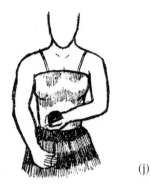

(j)

(1) Beats 1 and 2: Twirl the poi towards the body and catch it (diagram j).

(k)

(2) Beats 3 and 4: Twirl the poi sideways and catch in the LEFT hand (diagram k).

5 — PAKIHIWI (SHOULDER)

(l)

(1) Beat 1: Poi strikes the palm of the LEFT hand (diagram l).

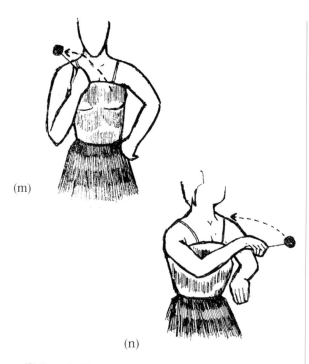

(m)

(n)

(2) Beat 2: The poi is swung up and strikes the back of the RIGHT shoulder while the LEFT hand rests lightly against the hip (diagram m).

6 — HURIHURI (SWING)

(1) Beat 1: Poi swung over the LEFT shoulder.
(2) Beat 2: Poi swung over the RIGHT shoulder.

7 — KAWAU (SHAG)

(o)

(1) Poi strikes back of the RIGHT shoulder (diagram o).

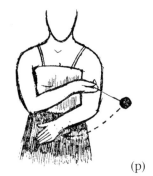

(p)

(2) Poi strikes back of LEFT hand (diagram p).
(3) Poi swings slowly back to the RIGHT shoulder, while the LEFT arm shoots out horizontally (diagram q). The poi travels away from the LEFT hand to the RIGHT shoulder in a spiralling movement which cannot be illustrated.

(q)

8 — WHAKAHONORE (SALUTE)

This is usually a concluding movement for a dance. The stance is as shown while the poi is twirled (r). There are variations, such as the poi hitting the RIGHT shoulder while the LEFT hand rests on the waist. Then the LEFT hand raises in salute as the RIGHT hand brings the twirling poi down to waist level.

(r)

DOUBLE SHORT POI — POI WAKA

The well known waka or canoe poi is a good example of double short poi. A version of poi waka (often called waka poi but in Maori the adjective follows the noun) is given below.

Words and Music

Toia mai nga waka e te iwi e	Haul the canoes, ye people
Hoea, hoea, ra!	Row them hard!
Aotea! Tainui! Kurahaupo!	These are the canoes!
Aotea! Tainui! Kurahaupo!	Bend your arms!
Hoea, hoea ra!	Bend your arms!
Toia mai nga waka e te iwi e	Paddle the canoes, ye people
Hoea, hoea ra!	Paddle them with a will!
Mataatua, Te Arawa! Takitimu! Tokomaru!	Not forgetting Mataatua, Te Arawa,
	Takitimu, Tokomaru
Hoea hoea ra!	Row them hard.
Haere mai e hine ma,	Come ye maidens come to me
Me nga taonga o te wa,	With your haunting melody,
Kia riterite ra te hoe,	Rowing forth in unity
Kia rere tika ai.	Till we reach our home.
Hoea ra te waka nei	Gaily our canoes shall glide
Hoea hoea ki te pai	Over the ever-swelling tide
Ma te poi e karawhiu	Twirling poi from side to side
Kia rere tika ai.	Till we reach the shore.

For the music of second half 'Hoea ra te waka nei' see the beginning of this chapter page 85.

THE MOVEMENTS

FIRST MOVEMENT

This consists of two actions illustrated below, each beginning on the first beat of a bar. The hands rest on the hips before the movement begins.

A — HOEHOE (Paddling About)

B — PAKIHIWI (Shoulders)

Both poi are together, alternately on the right side then the left.

For this movement both poi are swung over the same shoulder at the same time. When hoe is done to the RIGHT side pakihiwi is over the LEFT shoulder and vice versa.

The sequence of the movement usually is hoehoe right, pakihiwi left, hoehoe left, pakihiwi right and so on.

SECOND MOVEMENT — TOIA (Hauling)

The LEFT hand is placed on the shoulder of the woman in front.
The RIGHT arm moves backwards and forwards while the poi continues twirling.

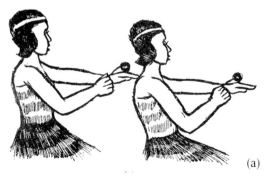

(a)

(b)

A – When the right arm is forward, a deft flick of the wrist causes the poi to hit the back of the left hand.

B – When the arm is right back, the poi is made to hit the back of the hand.

THIRD MOVEMENT— HOEA (Rowing)

Both poi are used and the arms are swing through a half-circle in a rowing movement. Both are twirled together. The end of the movement forward and the end of the movement back are accentuated by the poi hitting the ground at the front and at the back – each beat being the first beat of one bar of music.

(a) — Arms forward   (b) – Arms back

FOURTH MOVEMENT — HOEA ME PAKIHIWI

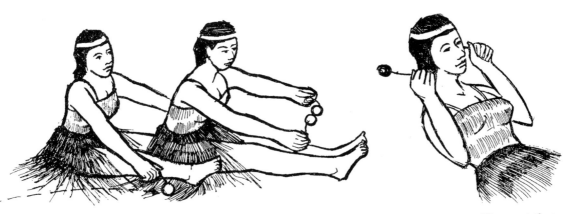

A — As for movement 3A.   B – As for movement 1B except that each hand is back over its own shoulder.

FIFTH MOVEMENT— HOPE

This is a simple variation of Movement 3A and it is not necessary to illustrate it.

A – RIGHT poi is brought forward so that it hits the ground near the RIGHT ankle while the LEFT hand is placed on the hip.
B – The RIGHT hand is brought back and placed on the right hip, while the LEFT poi is twirled down to hit the ground beside the LEFT ankle.

SEQUENCE OF THE POI WAKA

Movement	1A	1B	1A	1B
Words of song	*To* – ia mai **nga** wa – ka *e* te i – wi *e*…			

Movement	1A	1B	1A	1B
Words	*Ho* – ea *Ho* – ea **ra**… .			

Movement	2A	2B	2A	2B
Words	*A* – o – te – a **Tai** – nu – i **Ku** – ra – hau – **po** …			

Movement	2A	2B	2A	2B
Words	*Ho* – ea, *ho* – ea **ra**… .			

Movement	3A	3B	3A	3B
Words	*To* – ia mai **nga** wa – ka *e* te i – wi *e* etc. Continues to end of verse.			

Movement	4A	4B	4A	4B
Words	*Hae* – re **mai** *e* **hi** – ne **ma** …			

Movement	4A	4B	4A 4B
Word	*Me* nga, **tao** – nga *o* te **wa** … etc. Continues to end of verse.		

Movement	2A	2B 2A	2B
Words	*Ho* – ea **ra** te **wa** – ka **nei** …		

Movement	2A	2B	2A 2B
Words	*Ho* – ea, *ho* – ea **ki** te **pai** … etc. Continues to end of verse.		

Movement	3A	3B	3A	3B
Words	*To* – ia mai **nga** wa – ka *e* te i – wi *e* … etc. Continues to end of verse .			

Movement	5A	5B	5A	5B
Words	*Ma* – ta – tu – a! *Te* A–ra–wa! **Ta**–ki–mu! *To* – ko–ma–ru!			

Movement	5a	5B	5A	5B
Words	*Ho* – ea, *ho* – ea **ra** … .			

Syllables in italic type fall on the first beat of each bar.

102

12

THE ACTION SONG (WAIATA KORI)

As has already been pointed out in the introduction to this part of the book, the modern action song is the subject of a separate book of some length. Therefore the intention here is merely to outline its form and significance, followed by a few sample action songs.

Origin and Development

The action song is a modern development of the ancient haka waiata. This latter was a chanted song accompanied by actions which were neither as quick nor as energetic as those of the haka taparahi. An early writer, Dr Thompson, described a performance of the haka waiata as follows:

'Singing or the haka was the amusement of village maidens and young lads on fine evenings. For this purpose they assembled with flowers and feathers in their hair, and red paint, charcoal and petals of flowers on their faces. Most songs were accompanied with actions. The singers first arranged themselves in a row, the best voices commenced and finished each verse, then all joined in the chorus ... slapping one hand on the breast, raising the other aloft and making it vibrate with great rapidity. When the haka was sung by grown men, the singers stood in rows or squares.

The action of the legs and body was graceful, but the uplifted hands vibrating in the air during the chorus and the forced expirations and inspirations produced a singular wildness'.

It is interesting that this early account should make mention of men participating in the haka waiata, for today there are those who maintain that there is no historical sanction for men participating in action songs.

The essential difference, apart from the musical style, between the action song of today and the haka waiata of yesterday is that with the latter the actions themselves had only a rhythmic and artistic significance. There were only six basic actions, none of which had an intrinsic meaning. It was the words solely which conveyed the meaning and emotion. In the modern action song, however, the actions are completely complementary to the words and music since they mirror, and often intensify, the meaning of the words.

The first printed record of action songs as we know them today was in 1908. This was in the programme of the annual conference of the Young Maori Party whose leaders, headed by Sir Apirana Ngata, Sir Peter Buck and Sir Maui Pomare, were travelling among the Maori people preaching racial

"Hoatu i taku ringa"
(I give you my hand)

"Ka karanga ki te Matua"
(Call to the Lord above)

"Kei te moe tinana"
(My body is sleeping)

"Ki te reo o Wharepunga"
(The voice of Wharepunga)

103

pride, health and sanitation. To Princess Te Puea, however, goes the credit of organising the first touring concert party which featured action songs. A troop of Pacific Islanders who visited her at Ngaruawahia gave her the idea. Sir Apirana Ngata, always a progressive and far-sighted man, realised that the old waiata were rapidly passing out of favour with the young people, and he appreciated that if the old art forms were to survive, they must progress with the times. However, his attempts to give the haka waiata a new look were at first frustrated by the conservatism of his elders, who, understandably, were suspicious of any interference with the old ways. Thus it was not really until the First World War that Ngata was able to seize the opportunity to establish the action song firmly in the form in which we know it today. He used it prominently in the grand concerts which he organised all over New Zealand for the Maori Soldiers' Fund, and soon action songs were being performed everywhere.

During the Ngata and Te Puea era, certain conventions were set and strictly adhered to, particularly by the concert parties of Sir Apirana's Ngati Porou tribe. One such convention was the tame-tane approach for taking up a performing position. Based on sound historical precedent, it involved always approaching from the audience's right so that the left shoulders of the performers were towards the audience and their weapon hand, the right hand, was ready to swing forward freely should the occasion demand such an action. Another Ngati Porou convention was that the hand should never move across the face. A breach of this was regarded almost as sacrilege. This attitude has been considerably modified nowadays when there are a number of songs which include specific actions involving movement of the hand across the face. I see no objection to this provided that the face is only momentarily screened. A prohibition, particularly in the Taihauauru area on the west coast of the North Island, is not to have the palms of the hands facing outwards towards the audience. In olden times to raise one's palm

against a person meant to curse him. In modern times it may be said to be the Maori equivalent of thumbing one's nose at the audience, and hence unacceptable on the grounds of politeness.

These and other conventions were introduced partly because of historical precedent and partly because it was necessary to have some standard when teaching something new. There is often a tendency now to regard them as fixed and immutable. It is well to remember that any art form which is circumscribed by too many rules will lose its spontaneity. The action song is not a series of drill movements but a rhythmic expression of moods and emotions. Despite its ancient origins, it is essentially modern in its development and it must be allowed to evolve naturally. The criteria as to what is acceptable and what is not should be aesthetic rather than convention. It is for aesthetic reasons therefore that one can condemn such ugly innovations as the beating of the time with alternate feet, often affected nowadays by young performers, without being greatly concerned on the other hand by such matters as from what side of the stage a performing group might choose to enter.

The Music

In many action songs, the music is some popular European tune which has been adapted for the occasion. In others, the music, although European in style, is original, having been written around the Maori words of the song. This use of popular songs which often seems incongruous to Europeans, has been more fully discussed in the chapter dealing with Maori music. One essential, however, in my opinion, for an action song tune is an even, flowing rhythm. A recent trend towards the use of tunes which are a mixture of a rhumba, a samba and a pasa doble — with a bit of twist thrown in for good measure — has produced some bizarre results. Some people also seem to forget the word 'action' in action songs, and there is an increasing tendency to use tunes which produce languid, spineless actions. These are a poor substitute for the robust, tuneful and flowing music which is the hallmark of the great action songs.

Stance and Actions

For action songs, the performers stand in rows, usually with the women in front and men at the rear, although sometimes men and women may alternate in the same row. The leader stands apart or at the right end of the front row. He should not pass across the front of the performers.

Unlike taparahi actions, action song actions are flowing and without exaggeration or vehemence unless the words demand extra emphasis. In general, extravagant posturing is to be avoided. Wiri, or the trembling of the hands from the wrists (NOT just a wriggling of the fingers) is the mark of an experienced performer. Unless a special head movement is called for, the eyes follow the actions of the right hand.

There are certain differences between men's and women's actions. Most usual is in the 'hope' movement where the hands are placed on the hips. Men should rest the area between the thumb and forefinger on the hip with the fingers pointing forward. Women place the back of their hands on the hips. In actions which involve patting any part of the body, such as the chest or elbow, women merely caress the body, while men make a much more definite action which involves giving the chest, elbow, etc., a sharp slap more after the style necessary for haka taparahi. In some areas, women do not perform actions which involve revealing their armpits to the audience. Where such an action is required of the men, we may expect to see another action substituted for women performers.

Foot Movement

There are two distinct schools of thought in the foot movement for the action song.

In some areas, notably Taihauauru, the foot action consists of a rising on to the balls of both feet simultaneously in time to the beat (b). This produces a most graceful effect when used by all in a group. The most common foot action, however,

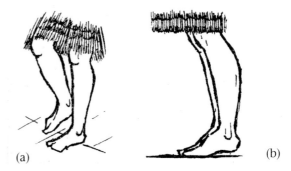

(a)   (b)

is a definite beat with the right foot leaving the ground while the body weight is taken on the left leg, the knee of which bends slightly in time to the beat (a).

For action songs in three-four or waltz time, the foot movement is more exaggerated, being a graceful swing of the lower right leg up behind the left knee. The right foot is 15 to 22cm off the ground at its highest point and the left knee bend is deeper.

A practice which is becoming increasingly prevalent is that of alternating the foot beat from one foot to another with each change of beat. This is unacceptable on both traditional and aesthetic grounds—particularly the latter. It will rarely be that an entire group uses this foot movement and even where such is the case it would be impossible to ensure that everyone uses the same foot at the same time. The result is a ragged, uncoordinated effect.

Correct foot movement is important and the technique has been illustrated and discussed at greater length in chapter 2.

105

Beginning and Ending an Action Song

There are a number of methods by which an action song may be started. The following is commonly used.

• The group stand with their hands to their sides.

• On the command from the leader, 'Kia rite' (ready) or 'Hope' (hips), the hands of all performers flash up together to the hips.

• The leader then sings a few bars of the song to identify it to the performers as well as to give the note for the music.

• The leader then calls 'Ringa e whiua' (swing the hands), and the hands are passed across the front of the body four times to the leader's call of 'Tahi, rua, toru, wha'. An alternative is 'Torona ki waho' (stretch out the arms), and the arms are extended in front of the body on 'tahi' and 'toru' and the chest patted on 'rua' and 'wha'.

• This establishes the tempo and the first action of

Hope!　　　　**Whiua**

the song begins.

To bring the actions to a close the leader calls on the final action, 'Tahi, rua, toru, wha' and the group calls 'Aue hei!' putting their hands on their hips on 'Hei!'

AN ACTION SONG – *ME HE MANU RERE*

Below is one verse of this very popular song and a simplified set of actions which are good examples of the way in which the actions illustrate the words in an action song. The novice should carry out the practice exercises in chapter 2, however, before attempting the action song with music. *Me He Manu Rere* came from North Auckland and was popularised some years ago when it featured in a British film on life in early New Zealand. For ease of learning, the version of the actions given here is much more simple than that normally performed with this song.

Me he manu rere ahau e	Had I the wings of a bird
Kua rere ki to moenga	I would fly to you while you were dreaming
Ki te awhi i to tinana	To hold you there and caress you
E te tau tahuri mai	My beloved turn to me

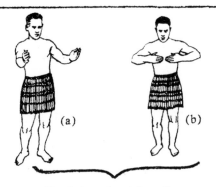

Hands in and out four times.

In time to first and third beat of each bar.

(a) A beckoning gesture. Palms of hand inwards.

(b) Pat the chest in time to the musical beat but the palms do not actually contact the chest.

Me he ma-nu re-re a-hau e
(Flying towards)

This action is depicted from the side. Actually the performers are facing the audience.

The hands are held pillow fashion behind the right ear and do not come in contact with the head.

The body is upright on the first beat of each bar then sways back with the right shoulder turning slightly to the right. Thus the body sways back a total of four times.

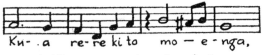

Ku-.a re-re ki to mo — e-nga,
(whilst you were asleep, dreaming)

(a) On the first beat of each bar the left arm and hand are closest to the body, as shown with the right hand on the outside.

(b) On the third beat of each bar the position is reversed, i.e., the right hand comes in over the top of the left so that it is closest to the body.

Ki te a-whi to ti- na ——na
(Holding caressing)

On "E", performers are facing the front with right hand outstretched to the right. Then in time to the beat performers pivot on the left foot, taking short steps with the right to finish facing left as shown above. An alternative is shown on the right. If men and women are alternated they can turn to face one another.

E te tau ta-hu-ri mai
(Turn to me)

ACTION SONG – *PAKIA KIA RITE*

This simple action song is reminiscent in its musical style of an ancient chant. It comes from the pen of the late Kingi Tahiwi who also wrote *Puru Taitama* in chapter 12.

Born in 1884 in Otaki, Kingi Tahiwi was a member of the Ngati Raukawa tribe. He was an interpreter with the Maori Affairs Department in Wellington for many years. He was one of the most prolific and versatile of modern Maori composers. He usually composed sitting in front of the kitchen fire plucking away at a banjo and then trying out the result on the piano. Sometimes he composed the music first. Other times he would play around with the words until he evolved a catchy lyric to which he might put his own music or one of the popular Pakeha tunes of the day. The result was a large collection of tuneful and often original songs which are sung and performed wherever Maori congregate.

A fine lyric tenor, Kingi Tahiwi and his brothers and sisters formed a popular vocal group, 'The Tahiwis'. Late in the 1920s this combination (without Kingi) went to Australia and made some of the earliest commercial recordings of Maori music. Kingi was one of the founders of the famous Ngati Poneke Young Maori Club of Wellington where 'orphan members' (as their theme song puts it) of tribes from all over New Zealand used to congregate to sing, play and dance during their years of work and study in the capital city. In 1935 a group which went from Wellington to Taranaki for the opening of the meeting house at Waitara called themselves 'Poneke' (the Maori translation of Port Nicholson which was the original name of Wellington). From this grew the Ngati Poneke Young Maori Club (Ngati means tribe) which was formed in the following year, 1936. It had an unbroken record stretching for over a quarter of a century. Kingi Tahiwi was one of the teachers and particularly encouraged Pakeha to come along to learn and perform with their Maori counterparts.

Kingi Tahiwi was a tireless organiser of patriotic concerts during the war years and in one year the Club under his direction staged over 200. For this and other services to the Maori people he was awarded the OBE. He died in 1948 on the eve of his retirement.

Pakia Kia Rite was composed in December 1937, and one of its earliest public performances was by the famous Waiata Maori Choir at a performance at Buckingham Palace in 1938 before King George VI.

Verse	E te iwi e! Whakaronga mai!	Hearken, o ye people!
	Me whai mai ta koutou i muri	Repeat after me
	I taku no reira	Wherefore …
Chorus	Pakia kia rite!	Strike your hands on your thighs
	Waewae takahia!	Stamp your feet!
	Ringaringa e torona kei waho hoki mai!	Stretch forth your arms then back
	Turi whatia! Hope whai ake!	Placing the palms on the chest
	Hei! Hei! Hei! Ha!	Bend the knee! Hands on hips!
Verse:	He mea pai ano	Tis good to be joyful
	Te ahuareka e	For it helps spread good cheer
	Hei ritenga e koakoa ai	Throughout those who are gathered
	Te minenga, no reira …	Wherefore …

E te i-wi e—— Wha-ka-ro-ngo mai ——

—— Me whai mai ta kou-tou I mu-ri

CHORUS

ta-ku No rei-ra.... Pa-ki-a ki-a ri-te waewae

ta-ka-hi-a ri-nga-ri-nga e to-ro-na kei wa-ho ho-ki mai. Tu-ri Wha-ti-a

Ho-pe wha-i a-ke Hei! Hei! He-i HA!

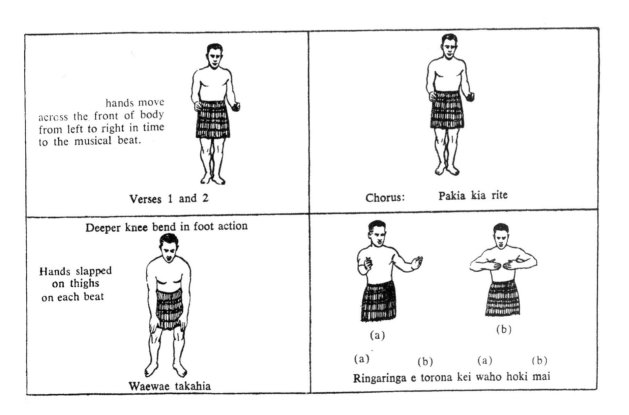

hands move across the front of body from left to right in time to the musical beat.

Verses 1 and 2

Chorus: Pakia kia rite

Deeper knee bend in foot action

Hands slapped on thighs on each beat

Waewae takahia

(a)   (b)

(a)   (b)   (a)   (b)

Ringaringa e torona kei waho hoki mai

From.....To twice Turi whatia	Hope whai ake
Hei	Hei	Hei	Ha

HOKI MAI E TAMA MA

This song has recently been revived in popularity by a well known group of singers under the title of *Hoki Mai E Tama Ma*. The original version, however, is *Tomo Mai E Tama Ma*. It was written by Henare Waitoa of Tikitiki (a small town 154km north of Gisborne on the East Coast) in 1945. The occasion was the opening of the Hine-pare Meeting House and Rangitukia, close to Tikitiki. Present at this function were a number of men of the Ngati Porou Contingent of the Maori Battalion, which had just returned from overseas, and the words of the song expressed greeting to these returning soldiers.

Tomo mai e tama ma ki roto (ki roto)	Welcome home, ye sons of war, oh welcome
I nga ringa e tuwhera atu nei	Welcome and enter my outstretched arms,
Ki nga morehu o te kiwi e	The sole survivors of the Battalion
Ki nga tama toa o tenei riri nui.	The brave sons of this great war.
Hoki mai! Hoki mai!	Welcome home! Welcome home!
Ki te wa kainga	Welcome our loved ones,
Kua tutuki te tumanako	Our hopes are now all fulfilled
Kei te kapakapa mai te haki	O'er the continent of Germany
O Ingarangi I runga o Tiamana e!	Now flutters the Union Jack.

Hoki ruarua mai e tama ma (tama ma)	Welcome home, ye few remaining braves of war
Ki nga iwi e tatari atu ne	Welcome home to your awaiting tribes;
Kua mahue atu ra nga tini hoa	Countless numbers of your friends now lie
Ki runga whenua iwi ke	Scattered through the many foreign lands.
Na te Moana ra ko te Wikitoria	It was Moana who gained the Victoria Cross,
Hei whakamaumaharatanga e	A perpetual reminder to us all
Ki o ratou tinana kei pamamao	Of those who in distant lands now lie
Ki o ratou ingoa kei muri nei	Whose names are now engraved within us.

The words of the more familiar *Hoki Mai* are given here with their accompanying actions. The tune is *Goldmine in the Sky* and is not reproduced owing to copyright.

Hoki mai e tama ma ki roto	Welcome home, ye sons of war, oh welcome
I nga ringa e tuwhera atu ne	Welcome and enter my outstretched arms;
Kei te kapakapa mai te haki	Now flutter the British flag
O Ingarangi i runga (o) Tiamana e!	O'er the lands of the enemy (Germany)
Hoki mai, Hoki mai	Welcome home! Welcome home!
Ki te wa kainga	To the familiar places
Kia tutuki te tumanako	So that our hopes may be fulfilled
Kei te kapakapa mai te haki	O'er the continent of Germany
O Ingarangi i runga (o) Tiamana e!	Now flutters the Union Jack.

111

twice

Hoki mai e tama ma

Ki roto

(ki roto)

Hands swung up from side (a and b). Then hands swing a circle from wrist in towards body (c). Clap (d) on "ri".

(a)   (b)   (c)   (d)

I nga   ri-nga

Palms pointing up. The hands are raised up to just above waist level beginning from a position about a foot below the waist.

On "nei" palms turn inwards and are swung across the body.

e tuwhera atu   nei

Fists swung across front of body.

Hands flicked upwards.

Hands flicked to
kapa—right
kapa—direct front
mai—left

Kei te   ka-pa   ka-pa   mai

Body sways from waist right, then left.

Te   ha-ki   (te ha-ki)

Circle and clap as in frame three. Clap on "ra".

Right fist circles under left elbow.

Inga-ra-ngi (i)   runga

Left hand on hip, right hand extended out in front with palm towards ground.

O Tiamana e

Each one twice
(total of four beats)

Hoki mai hoki mai

Ki te   Twice   wa kainga

E tu -   tuki   te tu -   manako

Fists swung
across front of
body.

Hands flicked
upwards.

Hands flicked
to
kapa—right
kapa—direct
front
mai—left

Kei te   ka-pa   ka-pa   mai

Body sways from waist
right then left.

Te   ha-ki   (te haki)

Hands swung up from side (a and b). Then hands
swing a circle from wrist in towards body (c).
Clap (d) on rangi.

(a)   (b)   (c)   (d)

I   - nga -   rangi

Right fist circles under left elbow.

runga

(o) Tiamana e

Left hand on hip. Right hand extended out to front
with palm towards ground.

(o) Tiamana e

NAU MAI RA E NGA IWI E

This is a more advanced action song than the three which precede it. It is brisk and vigorous, with a hint of haka taparahi in the emphasis and force of its actions. It expresses a theme prominent in many action songs — welcome, and an exhortation to the youth of the Maori race to treasure and to strive at the cultural heritage left them by their ancestors.

Nau mai ra e nga iwi e	Thrice welcome ye people
Ki runga o Aotearoa!	From the length and breadth of Aotearoa
Haere mai ra,	Thrice welcome,
Ki te whakarite i nga mahi	To this performance of the arts
O nga iwi o te motu.	Of the people of this land
Haere mai, haere mai,	Draw hither to the sounds
Haere mai ra.	Of my song of greeting.
Aue! Tainui, Horouta,	Let us this day remember
Mataatua, Kurahaupo,	The canoes of our forebears—
Takitimu, aue!	Tainui, Horouta and the like.
Hapaitia, aue hapaitia!	Take upon your willing shoulders
Nga mahi a nga tipuna.	The treasures of our ancestors.
Kia kaha ra, aue, kia kaha ra	Be ever steadfast and true,
Kei mate koe i te whakama.	And never ashamed of your heritage.

Hands moved across front of body left to right.

Nau   mai   ra   e   nga   iwi   e

Right hand moves once slowly across body from left to right.

Side view shown for clarity. Performers actually continue to face front.

Ki runga (o) Aotearoa

Haere mai ra

From ....To

Side view

I te whakarite nga mahi

O nga iwi o te motu

Haere mai! Haere mai!

Haere mai ra. Aue!

(a) Facing left and right alternately

(b)

Tainui	Horouta	Mataatua		Kurahaupo		Takitumu,		Aue!	
(a)	(b)	(a)	(b)	(a)	(b)	(a)	(b)	(a)	(b)
LEFT	LEFT	RIGHT	RIGHT	LEFT	LEFT	RIGHT	RIGHT	LEFT	LEFT

Arms go straight out in front of body with fists clenched on "tia". Hands open on "aue" and there is a sideways lunge of the body.

Ha...................tia   Aue

Arms out on "ti". Hands opened on "a".

Ha -   pai -   ti - a

The arms are swung up from the side (a) and (b) and then the hands swing a circle from the wrist in towards the body (c) and then clap (d). Clap is on "hi".

(a)   (b)   (c)   (d)

Nga   ma - hi

For "tipuna" hands move across the front of body from left to right in time to the musical beat.

a   nga   tipuna

(a)   (b)

four times.

Kia   ka..............ha   ra, aue   kia   ka - ha   ra...............
(a)   (b)   (a) (b)   (a)   (b)   (a)   (b)

116

Kei mate   Koe te whaka -   ma

Hands open on "ma"

PART FOUR

HAKA TAPARAHI AND PERUPERU

Introduction

In *Maori Action Songs*, Reupena Ngata and myself introduced a method by which we hoped that a novice could learn action songs from the printed page. We believed this to be possible because in the modern action song the actions are simple and, with the words, are tied to a rhythm imposed by the regular beat of music. The inflection and expression of the words is naturally governed by the tune. The haka, on the other hand, is very different from the stylised action song. It is disciplined, yet emotional. More than any other aspect of Maori culture, this complex dance is an expression of the passion, vigour and identity of the race. It is, at its best, truly a message of the soul expressed by words and posture —

Ko te haka he kupu korero
He mea whakairo e te ngakau
He mea whakapuaki e te mangai
He mea whakatu e te tinana

For this reason, I do not believe that the haka can be learned by the uninitiated with any degree of competence from diagrams on paper. The inflection of the voice, the changing facial expressions, the alternating syncopation of the words – often in subtle counterpoint to the regular beat of the actions – these just cannot be adequately conveyed by mere diagrams. In the hands of experienced performers, the haka is a composition played by many instruments. Hands, feet, legs, body, voice, tongue and eyes, all play their part in blending together to convey in their fullness the challenge, welcome, exultation, defiance or contempt of the words.

Nevertheless, if the novice feels so disposed, he should attempt some of the more simple haka depicted here. The book will help to achieve the first steps. There is, however, only one finishing school. That is to work as part of a group under a good leader.

I must plead for indulgence on the question of translations. Translating of haka is fraught with difficulty. There is often a great economy of language and some allusions take may lines to explain. In a book such as this, one can try a literal line for line translation and then explain the meaning in numerous footnotes. The other alternative is often criticised as unwarranted licence. This consists of framing the translation in such a way that the meaning is conveyed, but in so doing the English version bears little relation literally to the Maori against which it appears. Thus the first method is clumsy and the second misleading. I have tried to steer a middle course (which is always a dangerous thing to do). The translations try where possible to be literal. Where, however, the result would be obtuse, then I take shelter behind the abused phrase 'poetic licence'. This is not really a work for the scholar of the Maori language, and the main thing is that people performing haka understand generally what the emotions and thoughts are that they are trying to convey. I trust the translations therefore achieve this result for readers.

13

THE HAKA IN ANCIENT MAORIDOM

Terminology

The question of terminology has already been mentioned in the introduction to Part 3. As has been pointed out, the term 'haka' means simply a dance. Reference books give names for many types of haka performed in pre-European times in different styles and formations and for different purposes. These ranged from the haka waiata – the forerunner of the modern action song – to the extraordinary haka pirori – a haka of revenge and contempt in which the participants were completely naked and performed every posture calculated to insult and revile those against whom it was directed. Quite often the terms for the different types of haka had different meanings in different districts.

Common usage today restricts the word 'haka' to denote the shouted posture dance normally performed by men. Within this there are two divisions – the haka taparahi, which is performed without weapons and may express any public or private sentiment, and the peruperu, which is performed with weapons, and hence is usually warlike in character. This latter is not often seen nowadays and the haka taparahi is generally regarded as the true haka.

Other terms are also used which sometimes give rise to confusion. It should be pointed out that these terms denote the *purpose* for which the dance is used and not the *type* of dance. A 'ngeri' is a peruperu, the purpose of which is to exhort warriors before going into battle or commencing some noble endeavour. The 'tutu ngarahu' is a peruperu in which in olden times warriors were arrayed and inspected prior to battle. A taparahi which expresses mourning and is performed at

tangi is haka maimai. In this the women play a prominent part and use swaying motions of the body and arms known as aroarowhaki. Haka kaioraora is a taparahi of abuse or recrimination, such as *Te Kiringutu* given on page 149. A haka tutohu or turanga-a-tohu was once used for purposes of divination (tohu—a sign or omen). The performers were arranged in a wedge formation. This is not seen nowadays.

As was mentioned above, there are also a number of specialised terms applied to taparahi with special characteristics. These are now obsolete and I strongly suspect vary in connotation between tribal districts. Some examples of these are given for interest's sake. Haka horuhoru was performed kneeling, and for haka ruriruri the performers sat. During haka horuhoru the players also made deep grunting sounds, hence the name. For haka pikari certain leg movements were used that are not seen in other taparahi. The term pikari means to shuffle. Haka aroakapa is a taparahi performed in the formation common today, of two or more rows facing the same direction, in contrast to haka porowha, where the participants were in a square with the ranks facing four ways. This was presumable, suitable if the audience was arrayed on all sides and would be particularly useful when the audience's peaceful intentions were suspect. As has been mentioned, haka tutohu was one performed in a wedge formation. For other terms the reader is referred to the glossary at the back of the book.

Legendary Origin of the Haka

According to legend, Ra the sun god had two wives called Hine-raumati, the summer woman, and Hine-takurua, the winter woman. Ra had a son by Hine-raumati who was called Tanerore. During the calm, hot days of summer, when Hine-raumati is visiting this earth, it is possible to see a curious 'wiri' or trembling of the air, which the Maori will tell you is Tanerore performing for his mother. This dance of Tanerore performing is the origin of all the haka of this world, and in haka today the trembling of the performer's hands brings alive again the dance of the son for his celestial mother, Hine-raumati.

The first haka taparahi performed by mortal man was that of the people of the great chief Tinirau. Tinirau had a tame whale of which he was very fond. Unfortunately the pet was killed by a man called Kae. Tinirau was understandably incensed by this and sent a war party to look for Kae. None of this party knew the culprit by sight, so they were faced with the task of making him laugh, since it was said that Kae's teeth overlapped in a distinctive manner in front. (Some accounts say they were gapped in front).

After arriving at Kae's village, ostensibly on a friendly visit, some of the wormen of Tinirau's group offered to perform. They played games and instruments at great length but failed to arouse their audience to the desired gales of laughter. Finally one of the women jumped up and began to dance, but shouting the words instead of singing them and exaggerating the actions with much extravagant posturing. This really brought the house down, and at the end everyone laughed and clapped for more. It was then that Kae was recognised by his teeth. Later he was spirited away from the village and killed. Thus was the death of Tinirau's whale avenged and the first haka taparahi performed.

The Haka in Olden Times

Many accounts exist by early visitors to New Zealand of performances of the haka in all its original glory and power. Men were the usual performers but sometimes women took part, particularly in those which extended welcome and greeting. One early account of a war haka described it as being led by 'a painted harridan'. The men wore little while dancing and General Robley's famous sketch of a Maori warrior performing a peruperu shows him wearing a maro – a small triangular apron, the point of which was allowed to hang loose or was drawn up between the legs and fastened in rear. Sometimes they performed naked, but even so, the close lines of tattoo on their bodies gave the impression, as one observer puts it, that the men were clad in purple tights.

Before battle, the warriors would gather on the marae. The leader of the taua or war party would move out into the centre and call in a stentorian voice his whakaaraara pa:

Tika tonu mai
Tika tonu mai
Ki ahau e noho nei
Tika tonu mai
I a hei ha!

Come forth this way
Towards me,
To this place where now I stand
Come straight this way
I a hei ha!

At his signal the warriors would come forward and assemble for the tutu ngarahu, a peruperu which was by way of an inspection of the war party. During the dance the tribal elders would bend low and watch the feet. All performers had to be in the air together in the tremendous leaps of the haka, for disunity in the dance was an omen of disaster to follow. An offender who had his legs down when the rest were high in the air was sought out and castigated and perhaps even left behind in disgrace when the taua departed. If the omission was bad, or the occasion particularly portentous, he might even be struck down and killed on the spot.

The late Tuta Nihoniho, an officer of the Ngati Porou contingent during the Hauhau wars on the east coast of the North Island, wrote an essay containing advice to young warriors before going into action. He said (in Maori): 'Before you go into battle, show your legs to the women, young folk and old men in a tutu ngarahu. Your women will not fail to notice the omens of the dance, which lie in the correctness of posture or errors which you commit. When you see your womenfolk advancing with warlike faces by the side of your column, you will know that your legs will behold the stars above and the earth below. If, however, you should commit mistakes and not hold yourself correctly, then you will not see your women dancing because they will be full of apprehension. Thus if you realise you have made errors in your dancing, be cautious.'

Kaea:	Kia piri, kia tata te riri, te nguha e!
Katoa:	E ngana o niho
	Ki tona upoko
	Ki ona whekau
	Ka pau te marama e!

Let war and fury explode
Let your teeth sink
Into the enemy
Tear him asunder
Thus be the moon devoured

The tutu ngarahu would usually be followed with a ngeri, a peruperu which was an exhortation to the warriors. The ngeri which follows belongs to the Ngati Whatua and Te Roroa tribes of northern Wairoa. Visitors to the hinterland of the northern Wairoa River will see Tokatoka (literally rocks upon rocks) rising to a sharp crag from the eastern bank. In the early years of last century it was the home of the great warrior Taoho, chief of Ngati Whatua, and Te Uri-o-hau. This chant was used before the battle of Te Moremonui where Taoho and his taua defeated a mighty host of Ngapuhi under Pokaia.

Kaea:	Ae! Ko te puru e!
Katoa:	Ae! Ko te puru
	Ko te puru ki Tokatoka!
	Kia ueue!
	Kia tutangatanga i te riri,
	E kore te riri
	E tae mai,
	E tae mai ki Kaipara
	Ka puta waitia
	Aee-ae! Te riri!

Yes! This is the buttress!
Indead, it is the rock 'Puru'
The mighty rock of Tokatoka!
Be steadfast
Laugh at your foes,
The flood of battle
Shall not engulf us.
We who reside within the bosom
     of Kaipara Harbour
Shall always be brave!
Onwards to battle, victorious!

14

THE FORM OF THE HAKA

The Words

The words of the various haka run the whole gamut of public and private emotion and do not merely deal with warfare and exhortations to battle, as many people suppose. Welcome and farewell to visitors are popular themes. Haka can express a grievance or complaint, or even be a prayer addressed to one of the ancient Maori gods. Private sentiments include exultation at the act of love, and triumph at escape from capture such as in *Ka mate*. Elsdon Best remarks that often the excuses for composing a haka were very trivial and mentions one 'ridiculing a bush native who tried to eat a cake of scented soap!' Many ancient haka are unfortunately virtually untranslatable today either due to the fact that we have no knowledge of the incidents mentioned in them or because they contain obsolete or corrupted expressions. Consequently such haka are seldom performed.

Like much that is Maori, the haka has suffered from the influence of European civilisation. Often nowadays the words are indistinctly articulated and regarded as being secondary in importance to the actions. Vigorous actions to a mumbled refrain mean nothing. It is similar to pounding on the table with the fist and yet saying nothing. All haka are, as has been pointed out in the introduction, the expression of a message. The words convey the message and the actions are merely a vehicle for the words — a means of emphasis. If the message does not reach the audience, the whole performance is meaningless and sterile. Therefore, enunciation (whakahua) of both vowel and consonant must be clear and resonant, coming from the stomach and the chest and not just the mouth. Breathing (nga), phrasing (kama), and rhythm (rangi) are of the greatest importance. A good teacher should always spend a considerable amount of time on practising the words before actions are ever attempted. For further details on this the reader is referred to the chapter on teaching technique in Part 1.

The Actions

Haka were performed in a variety of formations and positions. A hollow square or a wedge shape was quite normal. Nowadays it is usual to perform with the performers in evenly spaced rows, although some authorities claim that a peruperu should always be done in a wedge formation.

The actions themselves differ from the action song in that they involve leaping and extravagant posturing, as well as facial grimaces, such as protruding of the tongue and rolling of the eyes. Constant performance of action songs has regrettably induced a tendency among young people to bring the gentility appropriate to this dance form into the actions of the haka. This must be quickly eradicated during rehearsal. In haka the sentiment expressed may well be peaceful, but the actions must still be vehement to convey the requisite heartiness and sincerity. They must be crisp, decisive and purposeful. Above all, the performers must perform in perfect unison. As has been pointed out in the previous chapter, this was indispensable in olden times.

Generally the eyes will watch the enemy (nowadays the audience). Sometimes, to draw attention to a particular action which stresses a significant point (such as the right hand going across the body towards the left elbow and back sharply to indicate tearing someone to pieces) the eyes will follow the particular action briefly and then move back to the audience.

The term for various body contortions are

pukana (rolling of the eyes), pikari (wild staring), whatero (protruding of the tongue), whakapi (grimacing, generally with the mouth) and aroarowhaki (wriggling the thighs and hips). The facial actions are a means of emphasis and an expresssion of fierceness and determination. They should proceed concurrently with the other actions. The practice of performers stopping in the middle of a haka to hold a prolonged pose while they contort their faces for audience belly laughs may provide comic relief but adds little to the dignity or meaning of a performance.

As has been mentioned, nowadays haka taparahi are usually done by men. Peruperu always are. Some taparahi, however, are designated women's haka. These are invariably used as powhiri or haka of welcome. Sometimes women will join in from their position behind the men in a haka performance, but they will not normally do all the actions which the men do. This is a far cry from the old days when an early visitor, Earle, writing in 1827, said 'I was astonished to find that their women mixed in the dance indiscriminately with the men and went through all those horrid gestures with seemingly as much pleasure as the warriors themselves.'

The Leader

The leader of the haka is similar to the conductor of the orchestra. He sets the rhythm and mood of the composition. He provides punctuation as well as guidance and inspiration to his team. The usual Maori word for haka leader is 'kaea', which also means, appropriately enough, the leader of a flock of parrots. Other words are 'kaitaki' and 'kai kakariki'. Few conventions bind the leader, who has something of a roving commission throughout the performance. One restriction, however, is that he should not move in front of the performing party at any time. Even in a haka taparahi the leader may carry a weapon such as a patu or taiaha to give emphasis to his role. According to Best, women haka leaders in olden times 'were noted for their lascivious motions of the onioni (wriggling) type'.

Rhythm

The haka is a supreme expression of the Maori sense of rhythm and timing. The Maori did not use drums or musical instruments as accompaniments for their posture dances. The sole beat comes from the stamping, in perfect unison, of the performers feet. Sometimes this beat changes during the course of the haka. Often the natural stress of the words runs counter to the beat of the actions. The beat has been marked in the haka which follow, but in the final outcome it is the haka leader who will establish the beat of the actions and their relationship to the words.

Marking the Rhythm

This key explains the marking employed in marking the beat of the haka which follow.

Ki – no or *kino* = beat falls on the syllable marked.

(beat or (--) = Beat falls during a pause in the words.

Inahoki (ra) te = The word bracketed, although necessary to the grammatical sense in the written version, is not sounded when the haka is performed.

(pu) huru = the syllable bracketed is not pronounced. Instead there is a pause in which the beat falls.

Kino .... = Indicates that the sound preceding the dots is prolonged. If written as kino (beat) it indicates that a beat falls during the period that the sound is prolonged.

Ko – i – a = Indicates that there is no elision of the syllables. Each syllable gets the same value, although the beat may fall on the first. Compare with the same word printed as *koia* which means that the whole word, as distinct from only the first syllable, is pronounced on the beat.

Stance

The haka stance is one of relaxed readiness, with the feet apart and the knees slightly bent so that the hands can reach the thighs without any sagging or bending at the waist. The shoulders are thrown back and open. Often young performers tend to grin. This looks bad. The expression should be vigilant, even fierce. The eyes fix the audience and the body remains motionless awaiting the kaea's first call.

Beginning a Haka

First the leader will order 'Kia mau!' or 'Kia rite!' (be ready) and all the hands will flash onto the hips together. For haka, the part of the hand between the thumb and forefinger rests on the hip bone.

The kaea may then begin the haka or order 'Ringa pakia' (slap the hands) and all hands beat on the thighs as illustrated. The feet may begin stamping but more correctly should await the call 'Pakia, pakia' or 'Waewae takahia' (stamp the feet). Once the rhythm has clearly settled down to the correct tempo, the kaea will give his opening call. If he is not satisfied, he may call a direction such

as 'Uma titaha' (throw out your chests) or 'Turi whatia' (bend the knees).

The foot action for the haka is dealt with in some detail in the chapter dealing with teaching technique and need not be repeated here. Suffice to say that the beat is heavier and deeper than in the action song. Crozet, an earlier writer, said: 'They frequently danced on the deck of our vessels, and they danced so heavily that we were afraid they would break through the deck.' The structures mentioned in chapter 12 in connection with the habit of beating the time with alternate feet apply equally to the haka.

15

HAKA WEAPONS

The term 'haka weapons' has been used merely to denote the fact that these are the particular weapons usually used in haka taparahi and peruperu. It must not be thought that these are the only Maori weapons or that the weapons described below are purely ceremonial or for dance purposes alone. In olden times they had a strictly utilitarian purpose.

The Short Club or Patu

These are used in the haka taparahi by the leader to give emphasis and importance to his role. Sometimes the dancers themselves carry them, but not to use them in specific actions, as in the peruperu, but rather as something to hold in the hand. Often these clubs are lumped together and called 'mere' but this is not correct. The three types of club most commonly used are illustrated below. The genuine article is made of stone, whalebone, greenstone or hardwood. Those used on the concert stage today are generally cut out of a block of wood on the bandsaw.

Spears

There are several types of spear. That used normally in dances is the koikoi, which is 185 to 240cm in length and pointed at both ends.

Long Club

These are more commonly used in peruperu than koikoi. Audiences generally think of them as spears, but they are designed not for throwing but for use in close combat in the manner of the old

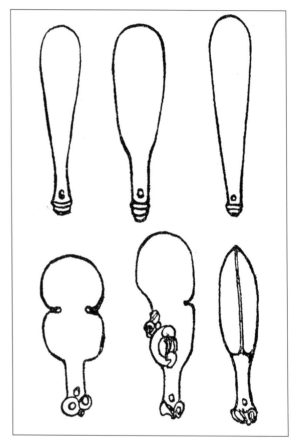

Short clubs or patu. *Top*: onewa (black stone), paraoa (whalebone), pounamu (greenstone).
Bottom: kotiate (whalebone), kotiate (wood), patuki (wood).

English quarter staff. The genuine article is about 152cm and made from a single piece of hardwood. Although all long clubs have basically a blade for striking and a sharp end for stabbing, they were made in different shapes – each with its own name. Illustrated are the two normally used in peruperu – the tewhatewha and the taiaha. The latter is the most common and dimensions of a typical taiaha are given so that groups can make their own if they so desire. Covered in a dark varnish they look quite realistic from a distance.

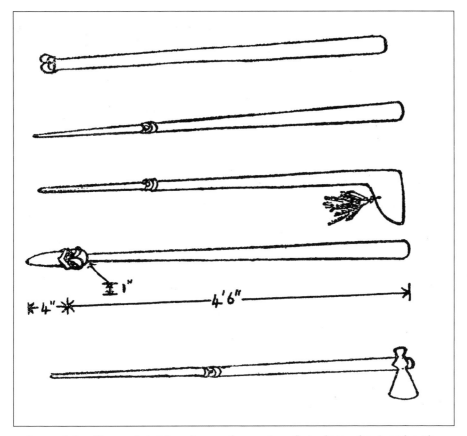

Long clubs. Hoeroa (whalebone), pouwhenua (wood) tewhatewaha (wood with feather ornament), taiaha (wood), toki kakauroa (wooden handle with trade axe-head used after the arrival of the Europeans).

16

POUTINI – AN EXERCISE HAKA

Poutini is one of the easiest haka and an ideal exercise for beginners, although it cannot be recommended for those who have let their waistline get out of order! The words are not complex, yet they teach facility in the Maori language. The rhythm is regular and strongly developed. The actions require little teaching and a novice group will pick them up quickly and thus gain in confidence. Nevertheless these actions serve to pinpoint a performer who is not in step with the rest. Thus it practises group coordination. I consider *Poutini* a good haka for the group leader to begin a haka practice and ideal for the learner after he has tried his hand at the series of practice exercises detailed in the chapter on teaching technique.

The words of *Poutini* have always presented some difficulty in translation and some of the most frequently performed versions are meaningless. It is doubtful whether the ancient Maori ever composed a dance to a complete set of nonsense words, hence those versions which are meaningless are no doubt corruptions.

According to one account *Poutini* was often used, and possibly even originally composed, as a harikai or food-bearing chant performed by the young men and women with special steps as they carried their baskets of food from the whare umu or cooking shed out onto the marae to lay them before the tribal guests.

Kaea:	Poutini! Poutini!	O star in the sky
	Ki to rua rere ha!	Fly away to your dark lair
Katoa:	Aue Kape! Aue Kape!	O wind of the North West
	Ki to rua rere ha;	Rush into the abyss of night
	Ue tama! Auaha ana!	Tremble, sons of men,
	Ue tama! Arahi ana!	Shake with passion
	Kss hei, kss hei	Yes we must go forward
	Kss hei ha!	Into the light of day.

Poutini! Poutini!
Ki to rua rere ha
Aue Kape! Aue Kape!
Ki to rua rere ha!
Ue tama! Auaha ana!
Ue tama! Arahi ana
Kss hei, kss he, kss hei ha!
Kss hei, kss hei, kss hei ha!

Hands passed across front of body.

Hope!

Poutini! Poutini!

Ki to rua rere ha!

Knees more bent, exaggerated foot movement whilst body and arms swing across from waist.

Aue Kape! Aue Kape! Ki to rua rere ha!

Turn left

Ue

face front clap

tama!

Face front looking up Flick fingers

Auaha

Turn right

ana!

Ue

Face front clap

tama!

Face front looking up Flick fingers

Arahi

ana!

Crouch

Kss hei.

Flick fingers

Kss hei

Kss hei

ha!

Crouch

Kss hei,

kss hei,

Flick fingers

Kss hei

ha!

Hi!

129

POUTINI – ALTERNATIVE VERSION AS A HAKA ENTRANCE

This is a version of *Poutini* which can be used as a haka entrance.

Using it—

Either the men in their rows move forward, line abreast through the ranks of the women.

Or the men move onto the stage or marae from the side in file. After 'hi' the leader gives 'Hurihia'

and the men turn and face the audience ready to begin their haka taparahi.

When moving forward, the steps are long and low (more so than in the illustrations below) and the body is crouched with the knees well bent.

The first four lines of the haka are exactly as for the version on the preceding page.

130

17

RINGA PAKIA — AN EXERCISE TAPARAHI

To Pakeha, *Ringa Pakia* is the best known of all haka for it has been constantly performed (and consistently mutilated!) by generations of sports teams, from the All Blacks downwards, performing it as a preliminary to some epic encounter. I would like to think that its inclusion here might ensure that in future it is performed, or at least its words rendered, in something approaching Maori style, but this I realise is a vain hope!

Although longer and less simple than many others, it can nevertheless be regarded as the basic haka. Maori and Pakeha children alike, learning the haka taparahi, take their first faltering steps to its words, and Maori concert programmes are seldom complete without *Ringa Pakia* either as an item on its own or as a lead-in or lead-out to some other haka.

Leader:	Ringa pakia!	Slap the hands (against the thighs)!
	Pakia, pakia, waewae takahia	Slap the hands, stamp your feet,
	Kia kino …	Look fierce …
All:	E kino nei hoki!	Indeed we are doing just that!
Leader:	E ringaringa e torona	Stretch forth your hands
	Ki waho mau tonu!	Hold them out to the furthermost horizons!
All:	Kss e!	We are!
Leader:	Tau ka tau!	Raise your voices in the war cry!
All:	Hei!	Yes!
Leader:	Tau ka tau!	For we have arrived!
All:	Hei!	Indeed!
Leader:	Tau ka tau ki runga o te marae	We have reached the marae
	Whangaia mai ra.	Offer us sustenance.
All:	Nge, nge, nge	Already we are panting with exertion
	Ara tu! Ara te! Ara ta!	Stand up! Breathe out! Breathe in!
Leader:	Ara whangaia mai ra!	Offer us help!
All:	Nge, nge, nge Ara tu! Ara te! Ara ta!	

Leader:	Ka tahi, ka riri, toru, ka wha	First, the challenge, thrice, even four times
All:	Homai o kupu!	Let us hear your words (of welcome)
	Kia wetewetea!	Unravel the knots which bind us
	Kss wetewetea! Kss wetewetea!	(For custom prevents us from entering the marae
	Kss! Ara tu! Ara te! Ara ta!	Until the welcome words are spoken!)

The rhythm is simple to master. There is an alternative syncopated beat which is more difficult. The beat suggested here gives a better defined action.

> Ringa pakia! (pause while beat is established)
> *Pakia, pakia, waewae takahia*
> *Kia* kino ... *E* kino *nei* ho*ki* (beat)
> *Eeeee* ringaringa e *torona* ki waho *mau* tonu
> Kss eh! (beat)
> Tau *ka* tau *Hei!* (twice)
> Tau *ka* tau *ki* runga (o) *te* marae
> *Whangaia mai* ra
> *Nga nge, nge!* Ara *tu!* Ara *te!* Ara *ta!*
> Ara *wha*ngaia *mai* ra! *Nge, nge, nge!* Ara *tu!* Ara *te!* Ara *ta!* (beat)
> Ka *tahi*, ka *riiiiii-ri, toru,* ka *wha*
> *Ho*mai *o* kupu! Kia wete*we*tea
> *Kss* wete*we*tea! *Kss* wete*we*tea,
> *Kss!* Aru *tu!* Aru *te!* Aru *ta!*

Note: It is essential that in the movement where the hands beat on the thighs, there is no bending at the waist. The trunk remains upright while the knees are slightly bent. The head must also remain up.

RINGAPAKIA

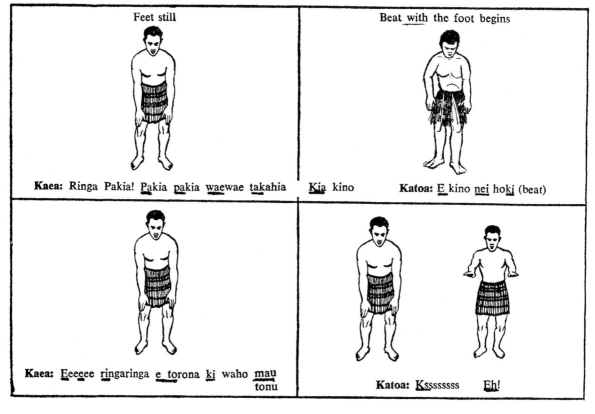

Feet still	Beat with the foot begins
Kaea: Ringa Pakia! Pakia pakia waewae takahia Kia kino	**Katoa:** E kino nei hoki (beat)
Kaea: Eeeee ringaringa e torona ki waho mau tonu	**Katoa:** Ksssssss Eh!

132

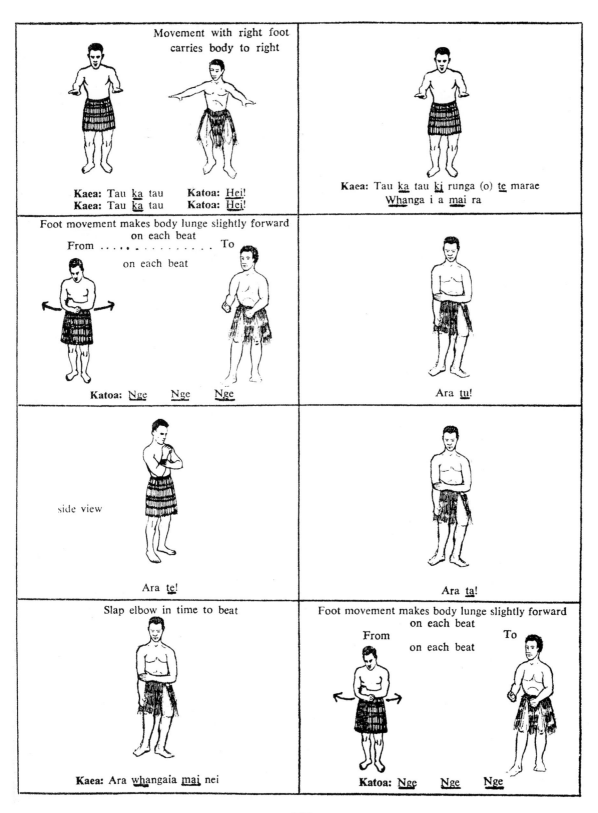

Movement with right foot
carries body to right

Kaea: Tau ka tau   **Katoa:** Hei!
Kaea: Tau ka tau   **Katoa:** Hei!

Kaea: Tau ka tau ki runga (o) te marae
Whanga i a mai ra

Foot movement makes body lunge slightly forward
on each beat

From . . . . To

on each beat

Katoa: Nge   Nge   Nge

Ara tu!

side view

Ara te!

Ara ta!

Slap elbow in time to beat

Kaea: Ara whangaia mai nei

Foot movement makes body lunge slightly forward
on each beat

From   To

on each beat

Katoa: Nge   Nge   Nge

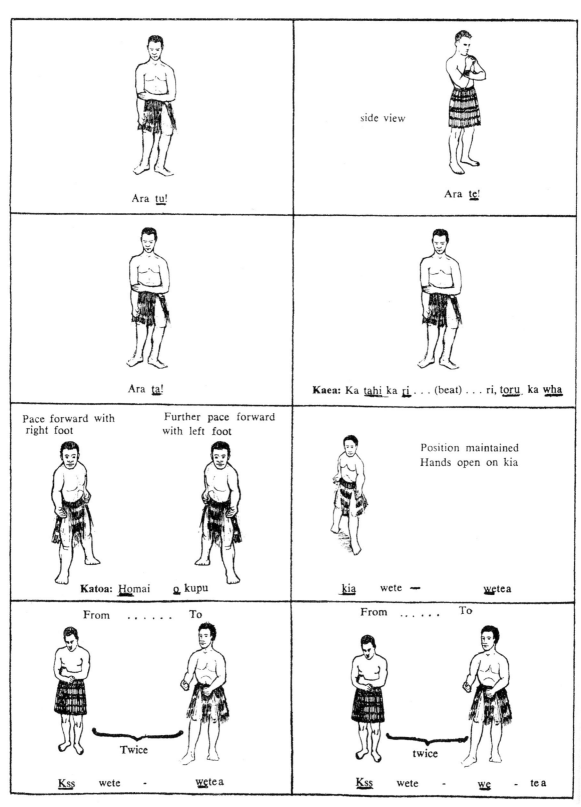

Ara <u>tu</u>!

side view

Ara <u>te</u>!

Ara <u>ta</u>!

Kaea: Ka <u>tahi</u> ka <u>ri</u> . . . (beat) . . . ri, <u>toru</u>, ka <u>wha</u>

Pace forward with right foot

Further pace forward with left foot

Position maintained Hands open on kia

Katoa: <u>H</u>omai <u>o</u> kupu

<u>kia</u> wete — <u>we</u>tea

From . . . . . . To

Twice

<u>K</u>ss wete – <u>we</u>te a

From . . . . . . To

twice

<u>K</u>ss wete – <u>we</u> - te a

134

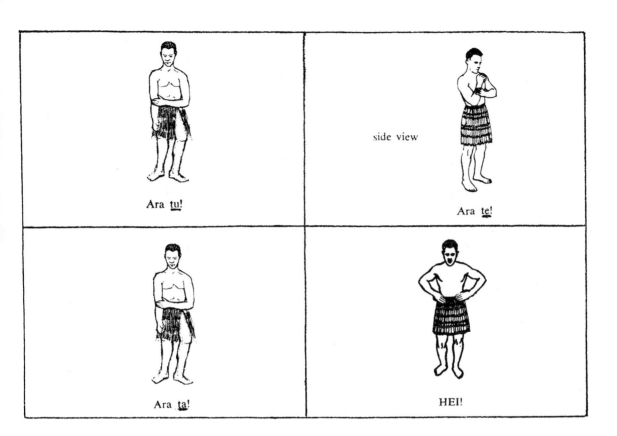

Ara <u>tu</u>!

side view

Ara <u>te</u>!

Ara <u>ta</u>!

HEI!

18

UTAINA

The chant which accompainies this haka taparahi is known as 'to (or tau) waka'. Any hauling song is termed 'to' and therefore 'to waka' is a time song used when dragging a canoe either to or from the sea. The same kind of chant was used to procure concerted action when a heavy ridgepole or stockade post had to be hauled into the pa from the surrounding bush. The metaphorical association which has caused such songs to be used to welcome people is not difficult to see. As the words thunder and echo across the crowded marae, the visitor knows that the canoe of good fortune is sailing before the wind and that all is well with the tribe and its guests.

Utaina!	Man the canoe!
Hei!	Yes!
Utaina!	Seize the paddles!
Hei!	Yes!
Utaina mai nga iwi	Put aboard the people
O te motu	Of this land
Ki runga o te waka	Into the canoe
E tau nei.	Floating here
A hikinuku e!	Thrust your paddles deep!
A hikirangi e!	Raise them now to the heavens!
A hikirangi e!	The paddles swing high!
A hikinuku e!	Now they dip low!
Ka hikitia e tana iwi	The people coax it forward
Ka hapainga e tana waka	The canoe is lifted on high
Aue! Aue! Aue ha!	Aue! Aue! Success!

RHYTHM	Kaea:	E Uta-i
	Katoa:	Na! *HEI*! (beat)
	Kaea:	E Uta-i
	Katoa:	Na! *HEI*! (beat)
		A *utai*na mai *nga* iwi
		O te motu
		Ki runga *o* te waka
		E tau *nei*
	Kaea:	A *hi*kinuku *e*!
	Katoa:	A *hi*kirangi *e*!
	Kaea:	A *hi*kirangi *e*!
	Katoa:	A *hi*kinuku *e*!
	Kaea:	i *a* ha *ha*!
	Katoa:	*Ka* hiki*tia ta*na iwi
		Ka hapainga tana waka
		*Au*e! *Au*e! *Au*e ha!

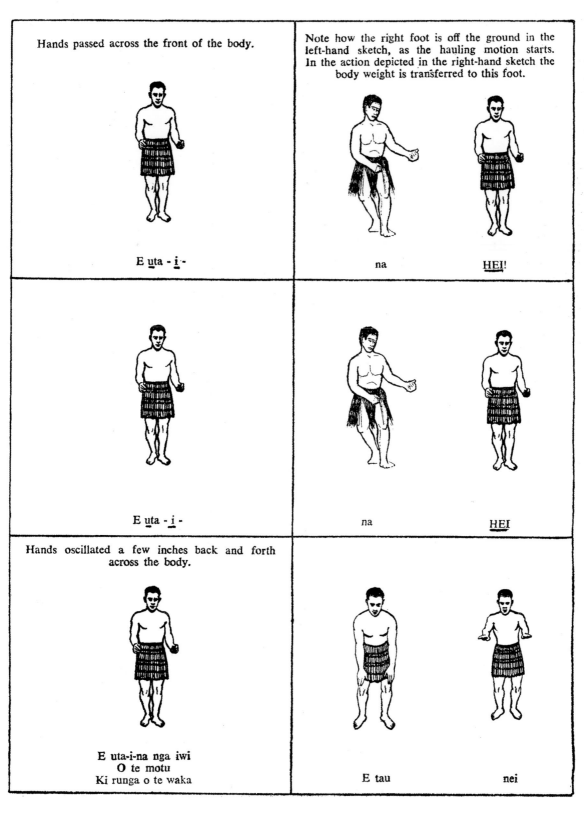

Hands passed across the front of the body.

E uta - i -

Note how the right foot is off the ground in the left-hand sketch, as the hauling motion starts. In the action depicted in the right-hand sketch the body weight is transferred to this foot.

na

HEI!

E uta - i -

na

HEI

Hands oscillated a few inches back and forth across the body.

E uta-i-na nga iwi
O te motu
Ki runga o te waka

E tau

nei

137

On the second 'hi' the right foot is momentarily off ground and body is "pumped" to the right. Weight is taken again on to the right foot on 'e'.

A <u>hi</u>ki nuku <u>e</u>   A <u>hi</u>ki rangi <u>e</u>

On the second 'hi' the right foot is momentarily off ground and body is "pumped" to the right. Weight is taken again on to the right foot on 'e'.

A <u>hi</u>ki nuku <u>e</u>   A <u>hi</u>ki rangi <u>e</u>

Hands slapped on thighs

(a)   (b)

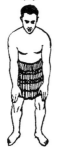

one action on each beat then repeat.

(a) (b)   (a) (b)
<u>Ka</u> hiki<u>ti</u>a   (e)   <u>ta</u>na <u>wa</u>ka

Hands slapped on thighs

(a)   (b)

one action on each beat then repeat.

(a) (b)   (a) (b)
<u>Ka</u> hapa<u>i</u>nga   (e)   <u>ta</u>na <u>wa</u>ka

<u>Aue</u>   <u>Aue</u>

<u>Aue</u>   <u>Ha</u>   HEI!

19

KA MATE! KA MATE!

Ka Mate is one of the best known as well as one of the most simple haka taparahi. It also has a very interesting history, for it is said to be only a portion of a long chant attributed to the famous chieftain Te Rauparaha. There is some controversy about its origin. Although the Tainui tribes are firm in their claims that it originated with Te Rauparaha, there is some evidence to suggest that the 'ka mate' portion at least was known in one form or other long before Te Rauparaha. It is, however, common Maori practice to freely adapt existing haka and waiata to a particular occasion, and Te Rauparaha may well have done this. One can envisage Te Rauparaha in his relief at delivery spontaneously bursting into a haka already known to him and adapting it as he went along.

History tells how Te Rauparaha went to Taupo to enlist assistance from Tuwharetoa against his troublesome neighbours, Waikato and Ngati Maniapoto. (See *Tuwharetoa* by John Grace). He was unsuccessful in this and decided to make for Taupo. While moving around the eastern shore of the lake he was almost ambushed by an enemy tribe who were lying in wait for him. Pursued by his enemies, the warrior chief arrived at Motuopuhi and appealed to the protection of the local chief, Te Whareangi. At first the latter was at a loss as to his best course of action. Finally he told Te Rauparaha to get into a rua kumara, or kumara storage pit, and then his wife, an old woman named Te Rangikoaea, sat on a mat covering the wooden lid of the pit.

The pursuing chiefs meanwhile were reciting chants which would locate their quarry and prevent him from escaping. As Te Rauparaha crouched in the inky darkness he felt 'mate Maori', the Maori sickness, creeping over him and turning his limbs to water as the spells took

effect. However, Te Wharerangi had foreseen this possiblity, and in instructing his wife to sit above the hunted chief he had utilised the power which she as a woman had on magical spells. Thus it was that Te Rauparaha now felt the evil effect of the incantations, which were swirling around inside the hole, being absorbed by the body of the old chieftainess above him, and he exclaimed.

> A ha ha!
> Kikiki kakaka kauana!
> Kei waniwania taku tara.
> Kei tarawahia, kei te rua i te kerokero!

Then Te Rauparaha become worried that the arrival of the enemy war party could disturb his protector:

> He pounga rahui te uira ka rarapa;
> Ketekete kauana to peru kairiri.
> Mau au e koro e Hi! Ha!
> Ka wehi au ka matakana.
> Ko wai te tangata kia rere ure
> Tirohanga nga rua rerarera
> Nga rua kuri kakanui i raro!

> Let neither trespass of foes nor the fury of
> nature
> Disturb your hostile intent towards the enemy,
> Remain faithful to me old one,
> Protect me! Be wary!
> (Very free translation)

The pursuers burst into Te Whareangi's village and demanded to know whether he had seen Te Rauparaha. The old chief hesitated and, listening in anguish below, Te Rauparaha whispered to himself. 'Ka mate! Ka mate!' (it is death for me). Then Te Wharerangi told the enemy that their quarry had fled on to the desert wastes of Rangipo and Te Rauparaha relaxed, 'Ka ora, ka ora!' (I live). But the enemy were not satisfied and they demurred, while the warrior chief again muttered 'Ka mate, ka mate!'

Finally they were convinced and rushed out of the village again in pursuit. Te Wharerangi threw aside the cover and as the sunlight flooded into the dark pit, Te Rauparaha sprang to his feet with a cry of exulation:

Ka ora! Ka ora!
Tenei te tangata puhuruhuru
Nana nei i tiki mai whakawhiti te ra
I live! I live
Behold the brave man
Who has caused the sun to shine again.

Ka mate! Ka mate!
Ka ora! Ka ora!
Ka mate! Ka mate!
Ka ora! Ka ora!
Tenei te tangata puhuruhuru,
Nana nei i te tiki mai,
Whakawhiti te ra!
Aue upane! Aue kaupane!
Aue upane, kaupane
Whiti te ra!

He climbed up the primitive ladder, which consisted merely of a log with notches (upane) until finally he reached the top (kaupane).

Aue upane! Aue kaupane!
Upane! Kaupane!
Whiti te ra!'
Up the ladder
Up and up
Into the light of the sun

Then going out onto the marae of the chief who had saved him, Te Rauparaha performed for the first time the haka of triumph and exulation which more than a century later still thunders across the marae of New Zealand on ceremonial occasions great and small.

Kaea:	*Ka* mate! *Ka* mate!
Katoa:	*Ka* ora! *Ka* ora!
Kaea:	*Ka* mate! *Ka* mate!
Katoa:	*Ka* ora! *Ka* ora!
	*Te*nei te *ta*ngata *pu*huru (beat) huru
	*Na*na nei i tiki *mai*,
	Whaka*w*hiti te *ra*!
	Aue *upa*...ne! Aue k*aupa*...*ne*!
	Aue *upa*ne, ka*u*pane
	*Wh*iti te *ra*!

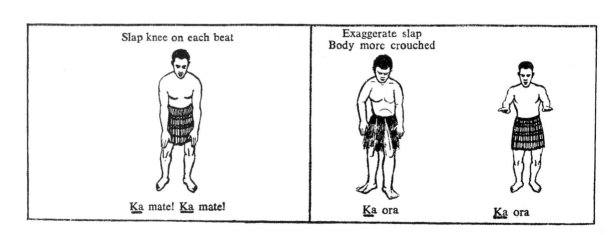

Slap knee on each beat

Ka mate! Ka mate!

Exaggerate slap
Body more crouched

Ka ora

Ka ora

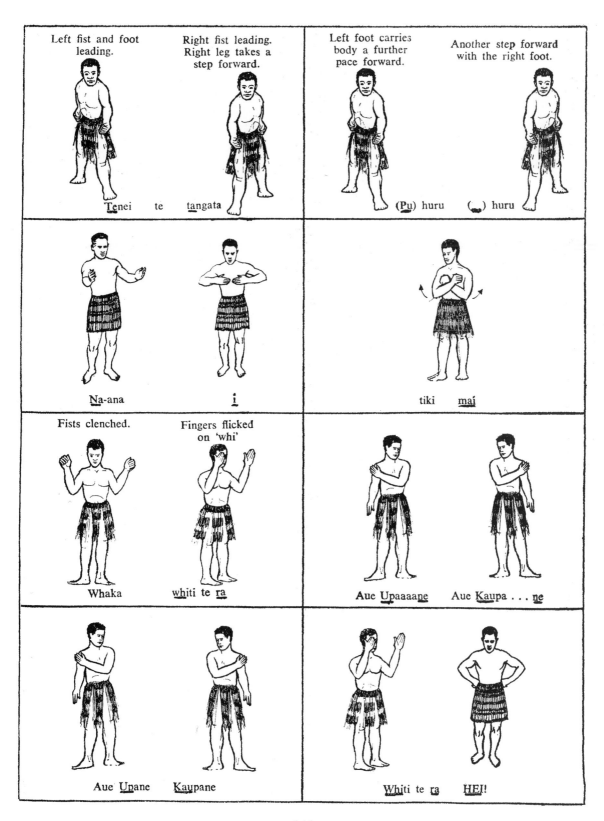

Left fist and foot leading.

Right fist leading. Right leg takes a step forward.

Left foot carries body a further pace forward.

Another step forward with the right foot.

Tenei   te   tangata

(Pu) huru   ( ) huru

Na-ana   i

tiki   mai

Fists clenched.

Fingers flicked on 'whi'

Whaka   whiti te ra

Aue Upaaaane   Aue Kaupa . . . ne

Aue Upane   Kaupane

Whiti te ra   HEI!

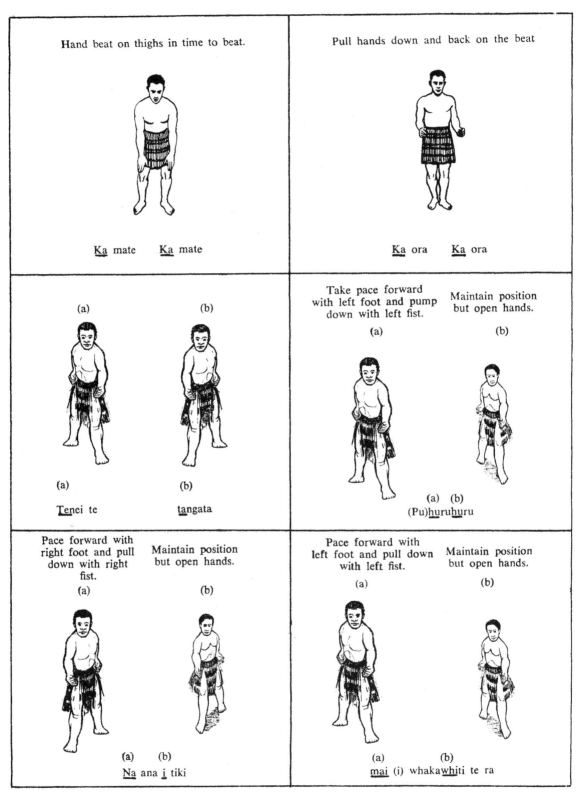

Hand beat on thighs in time to beat.

<u>Ka</u> mate   <u>Ka</u> mate

Pull hands down and back on the beat

<u>Ka</u> ora   <u>Ka</u> ora

(a)   (b)

(a)   (b)

<u>Te</u>nei te   <u>ta</u>ngata

Take pace forward with left foot and pump down with left fist.
(a)

Maintain position but open hands.
(b)

(a) (b)
(Pu)huru<u>hu</u>ru

Pace forward with right foot and pull down with right fist.
(a)

Maintain position but open hands.
(b)

(a)   (b)
<u>Na</u> ana <u>i</u> tiki

Pace forward with left foot and pull down with left fist.
(a)

Maintain position but open hands.
(b)

(a)   (b)
<u>mai</u> (i) whaka<u>whi</u>ti te ra

142

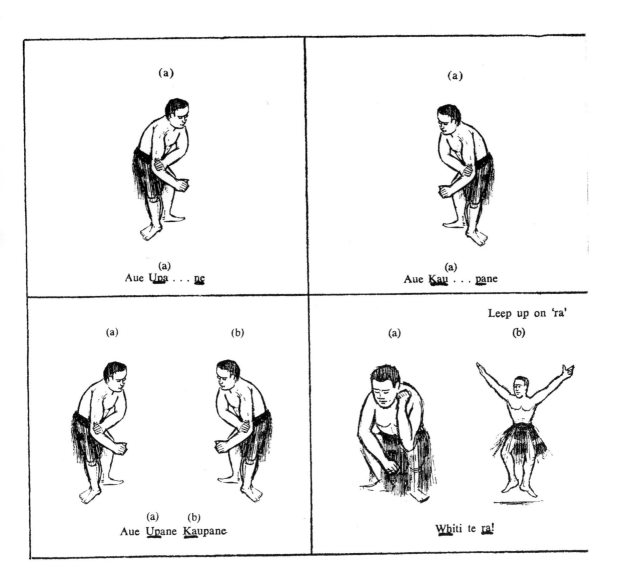

(a)

(a)

Aue Upa . . . ne

(a)

Aue Kau . . . pane

(a)   (b)

(a)   (b)

Aue Upane Kaupane

(a)   Leep up on 'ra'
(b)

Whiti te ra!

20

RUAUMOKO — THE EARTHQUAKE GOD

This complex and stirring haka is a North Island East Coast classic and the Ngati Porou tribe may justly be called its greatest exponents. The haka is thought to have been composed in the eighteenth century but may have originated much earlier, for legend describes it as being one of those performed by Ngati Porou before sallying into battle. According to the late Tuta Nihoniho, this was the war song chanted by Ngati Porou before their first engagement with the Hauhau forces of Te Kooti in 1865. Unfortunately a mistake was made in its rendition. According to ancient belief, mistakes in performing haka before battle were a very bad omen. So it proved to be in this case for the error foretold the death of several members of the force in the fighting which followed.

When revived by the Ngati Porou in 1901, *Ruamoko* was one of the highlights of the great Maori reception to the Duke and Duchess of York in Rotorua. Twenty years later it was again prominent at the Maori welcome in the same place for the then Prince of Wales. From being the specialty of a particular tribe, the haka now became the property of Maoridom as a whole and in 1934 a Nga Puhi party from North Auckland gave a masterly performance before Lord and Lady Bledisloe at the celebrations of Waitangi.

Anyone who studies the words to this haka will be aware of two levels of meaning. This use of a sexual theme is not unusual in haka.

Kaea:	Ko Ruaumoko e ngunguru nei!	Hark to the rumble of the Earthquake God!
All:	Au! Au! Aue ha!	Au! Au! Aue ha!
Kaea:	Ko Ruaumoko e ngunguru nei!	It is Ruaumoko who trembles and sits!
All:	Au! Au! Aue ha!	Au! Au! Aue ha!
Kaea:	A ha ha!	A ha ha!
All:	E ko te rakau a Tungawerewere! A ha ha!	It is the wand of Tungawerewere! A ha Ha!
	He rakau tapu, na Tutaua ki a Uenuku	The sacred rod given by Tutaua to Uenuku
	I patukia ki te tipua ki o Rangitopeka	It struck the monster Rangitopeka
	Pakaru te upoko o Rangitopeka	And smashed the head of Rangitopeka
	Patua ki waenganui o te tau ki Hikurangi	Cleaving the twin peaks of Hikurangi.
	He toka whakairo, e tu ake nei,	From where the carved rock emerges
	He atua! He tangata! He atua! He tangata Ho!	It is divine, yet it is of man,
Kaea:	He atua, he atua, Taupare-taitoko,	Yet it is divine
	Kia kitea e Paretaitoko te whare haunga!	Behold! It is the dark mystery of the womb!
All:	A ha ha! Ka whakatete mai o rei, he kuri! Au!	Where the dogs gnash their teeth.
Kaea:	A ha ha!	A ha ha!
All:	Na wai parehua taku hope kia whakaka te rangi	In my ecstasy I see the sky inflamed
	Kia tare au!	I gasp for breath

Kaea:	He roha te kawau
All:	Hei ha!
Kaea:	Kei te pou tara
All:	Tu ka tete, ka tete! Tau ha!
Kaea:	Ko komako, ko komako!
All:	E ko te hautapu e rite ki te kai na Matariki
	Tapareireia koia tapa!
	Tapa kononua koiana tukua! I aue! *

'Tis like a shag soaring on high
Hei ha!
As the rod drives deep
Thus it remains
Now it is the bellbird singing
Even though I am quiescent as in death
I soar amongst the stars.

RHYTHM

The rhythm of *Ruaumoko* is very difficult to render on paper. It is capable of considerable variation, particularly in the kaea's parts.

E (two beats) Ko Ruaumoko e ngunguru nei
Au! Au! Aue Ha!
E (beat) Ko Ruaumoko e ngunguru nei!
Au! Au! Aue Ha!
A ha ha!
E ko te rakau a Tungawere-we re!
A ha ha!
He rakau tapu (na) Tutaua ki (o) a Uenuku
I patukia (ki) te ti-puaki (o) Rangitopeka
Pakaru te upoko (o) Rangitopeka
Patua ki waenganu (i) o te tau ki Hikurangi
He toka whakairo, e tu ake nei,
He atua! ( ) He tangata ( ) He atua ( ) He
    tangata Ho! ( )
Hea-tuahea-tua Taupare-taitoko

Kia kitea e Paretaitoko te whare haunga (beat)
    A ha ha
Ka whakatete mai o rei, he kuri au! A ha ha!
Na wai parehua taku hope (kia) wha kaka te rangi.
Kia tare au! Hei! Ha! (beat)
He roha te kawau
Hei ha! Kei te pou tara
Tu ka tete, ka tete! Tau ha!
Ko komako, ko komako OR Ko koma… ko ko koma
    (ko)
(E) ko te hautapu e rite ki te kai na Mata…riki
Pakia! (beat) Tapareireia koi koia tapa (beat)
Tapa kononua koiana tukua
I au-e Hei

* The version above is the 1901 version of the words. It was adapted from the ancient forms by the late Mohi Turei of Ngati Porou.

Kia whakanga hoki au i ahau!

Kss aue!

E . . . Ko Ruamoko e ngunguru nei!

From . . . . To

Au! Au!   Aue Ha!

Ko Ruaumoko e ngunguru nei!

From . . . . To

Au! Au!   Aue Ha!   A ha ha

E ko te rakau a Tungawerewere! A ha! Ha!

(a)   (b)

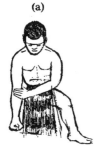

(a)   (b)

He rakau tapu (na) Tutaua ki (a) Uenuku

I Patukia (ki) te tipua ki (o) Rangitopeka

146

Slap the top of the LEFT hand. The LEFT hand is held above the right elbow and does not touch it.

Pakaru te upoko (o) Rangitopeka

Patua ki waenganu(i) o te tau ki Hikurangi
He toka whakairo, e tu ake nei

Chest is patted twice in each movement.

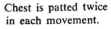

HO!
(full throated)

twice

He atua! He tangata! He atua! He tangata HO!

Turn slowly to finish line facing LEFT.

(—) He atua, he atua Taupare-taitoko

twice
Kia kitea e Paretaitoko te whare haunga—A ha ha

 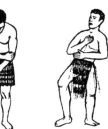

KA!
(face front)

Open on mai
Bite out the "au"

Ka whakatete mai o rei, he kuri au! A! ha ha!

Na wai parehua taku hope (kia) whakaka te rangi.
Kia tare au!

Fists clenched. Hands open on "wau".

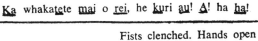

Hei!   Ha! (—) E roha te kawau

147

Face front.

Hei   ha   Kei te pou tara

Frequently performers are seen in this action bobbing up and down. This is wrong. With each beat the right foot is carried out for a distance of three inches so the effect is of the whole group of performers sinking lower.

From . . . . . To

Tu ka tete, ka tete

Clap.   Hand open.

Tau!   Ha!

Body straight up again.

Ko komako   Ko komako

(beat) Ko te hautapu e rite ki te kai na Matariki

Clap.

Pakia (beat) Tapareireia koi tapa!

Clap.

(beat) Tapa konunua kojana tukua

I au-e   HEI!

148

21

TE KIRINGUTU

This classic haka taparahi has its roots well into the past but in recent times, with the words adapted to suit the occasion, it has occupied a place of honour at many great Maori gatherings. With the words give below it was led by Tuta Nihoniho at the opening in 1868 of the original 'Porourangi' meeting house in the fertile Waiomatatini Valley on the East Coast of the North Island, eighty miles north of Gisborne. It was revived again in 1934 for the Waitangi celebrations before the Governor-General, Lord Bledisloe. At the beginning of the Second World War, men of the ninth and tenth reinforcements of the Maori Battalion featured it before their departure overseas at the opening of another famous meeting house, 'Tamatekapua' at Ohinemutu, Rotorua. Later still it was the contribution of the men of the lower Waiapu Valley and North Waiapu at the memorable gathering at Whakarua Park, Ruatoria, on 6 October 1943, when Sir Cyril Newall presented the Victoria Cross to the father of the great Maori warrior Second Lieutenant Moana-Nui-a-Kiwa Ngarimu.

Although the words given below are still used today when the haka is performed, they are a product of a bygone period of Maori-Pakeha relations. They were adapted in 1887 by Tuta Nihoniho from an earlier version of the haka. Nihoniho was a famous chief of the Hikurangi subtribes of the Ngati Porou people. At the time he was engaged in complicated litigation over the question of land. The judgment went against him and Ngati Porou tell that has it that after he left the courtroom in anger he composed this half-bitter, half-quizzical denunciation of the Pakeha and his complicated laws which had made the path so steep for a people struggling at that time to adjust to the demands of an alien civilisation.

In Tutu Nihoniho's original composition he used the word 'kamupene' (a transliterated version of the word company) instead of 'hoariri' (enemy) in the fifth line of the body of the taparahi. This referred to a current bogey, the British Land Company, a group of British speculators formed to buy Maori land on a large scale. The company purchased a considerable amount of land in the Gisborne area, where it was actively assisted by Wi Pere, then Member of Parliament for Eastern Maori. Tuta was very concerned at the company's invasion of Maori land and some authorities claim that this fact in itself is the raison d'être for the haka and not Tuta's failure in litigation.

Whakaara

Kaea: Ponga ra! Ponga ra!
All: Ka tataki mai te Whare o Nga Ture
        Ka whiria ra te Maori! Ka whiria!
        E ngau nei ona reiti, e ngau nei ona taake!
        Aha ha! Te taea te ueue! i aue! Hei!
Kaea: Patua i te whenua!
All: Hei!
Kaea: Whakataua i nga ture
All: Hei!

The Rising

The darkness presses all around!
The House which enacts the laws ensnares me
The Maori is plaited in its bonds! Brought low!
Its rates and its taxes gnaw at my vitals
Alas! It cannot be shaken!
The land will be engulfed
Hei!
Submerged beneath these laws!
Hei!

Na nga mema ra te kohuru

Na te Kawana te koheriheri!
Ka raruraru nga ture!
Ka raparapa ki te pua torori! I aue!

Taparahi

Kaea: Kaore hoki te mate o te whenua e
      Te makere atu ki raro ra!
All: A ha ha! Iri tonu i mai runga
      O te kiringutu mau mai ai,
      Hei tipare taua ki te hoariri!
      A ha ha! I tahuna mai au
      Ki te whakahere toto koa.
      E ki te ngakau o te whenua nei,
      E ki te koura! I aue, taukuri, e!
Kaea: A ha ha!
All: Ko tuhikitia, ko tuhapainga
      I raro i te whero o te Maori! Hukiti!
Kaea: A ha ha!
All: Na te ngutu o te Maori, pohara, kai-kutu,
      Na te weriweri koe i homai ki konei?
      E kaore i ara,
      I haramai tonu koe ki te kai whenua
      'Pokokohua! Kauramokai! Hei!
Kaea: A ha ha!
      Te puta atu hoki
      Te ihu o te waka i nga torouka o Niu
        Tireni
      Ka paia pukutia e nga uaua o te ture a te
        Kawana!
      Te taea te ueue! Au! Au! i aue!

From the members of the House has come this
    treacherous act
The Governor has aided and abetted them.
The laws are confused
Even the tobacco leaf falls victim to them!

The Taparahi Proper

The loss of our land
Bears on us like the hand of death!
Alas! Heard continually
Are the sinister discussions, clinging fast
As does the warrior's headband before the enemy!
Alas! I am seared and burned
By the sacrifice of blood
It goes to the heart of the land
I am indeed sorely distressed.
A ha ha!
We are raised aloft by promises
Even as we are put aside!
It is so
Was it not your promise to teach the Maori?
And wean him from his primitive ways?
Yet you come as marauders
To devour our land
No insult can express my contempt!
Alas!
How can the bow of our canoe
Forge past the headlands of New Zealand?

Obstructed as it is by the laws
Of the government
Alas! They cannot be shaken!

RHYTHM
Whakaara
Ponga ra! Ponga **ra**! A ha **ha**!
Ka tataki mai **te** Whare o **Nga** Ture
Ka whiria (**ra**) te **Ma**-ori! Ka whiria! (beat)
E ngau **nei** ona reiti (beat) e ngau **nei** ona ta**a**ke!
A ha **ha**! **Te** taea te ueue! (beat) **I** aue **Hei**!
Patua i **te** whenua! **Hei**! (beat)
Whakataua **i nga** ture! **Hei**! A ha **ha**!

Na nga Mema ra te kohu (beat) ru
Na te Kawana te koheriheri (beat)
Ka raruraru nga ture (beat)
(beat) Ka raparapa ki te pua torori! I aue!

Taparahi

(Two beats) Kaore hoki te mate o te whenua e
Te makere atu ki raro ra!
A ha ha! Aue! Iri tonu mai runga
(O) te kiringutu mau mai ai,
Hei tipare taua ki te hoariri! A ha ha
I tahuna mai au ki te whakahere toto koa.
E ki te ngakau o te whenua nei,
(E) ki te korua! (i) aue! taukuri e (beat) A ha ha!
Ko tuhikitia, ko tuhapainga,
I raro i te whero o te Ma... (beat) ...ori!
Hukiti! A ha ha!
Na te ngutu o te Maori, pohara, kai-kutu,
(Na) te weriweri koe i homai ki konei?
(E) kaore i ara (i) haramai tonu koe ki te kai
whenua!
(beat) Pokokohua (beat) kauramokai! Hei!
(beat) A ha ha!
Te puta atu hoki
Te ihu o te waka i nga (beat) toruka a Niu Tireni
Ka paia pukutia (e) nga uaua o te ture a te Kawana
Te taea te ueue! (beat) Au! (beat) Au! (beat) Aue Hei!

Right fist circles over the head and body leaps off the ground prior to going down into the third position (on the right knee).

Kia whakangawari au i ahau

No body movement.

Ponga ra Ponga ra! A ha ha!

151

Slap right fist on ground on 'ka' Assume position on 'ta-taki' Clench fists on 'Ture'

Hands open on 'whi' Fists clench on 'Ma' and revolve around one another on 'whi'

<u>Ka</u> tata<u>ki</u> mai <u>te</u> whare o <u>nga</u> Ture

<u>Ka</u> whiria (<u>ra</u>) te <u>Ma</u>-ori! <u>Ka</u> whiria! (—)

E ngau <u>nei</u> ona <u>rei</u>ti (—)

E ngau <u>nei</u> ona <u>taa</u>ke

<u>A</u> ha <u>ha</u>

Twice
From . . . . To
(a)   (b)

(a) (b)   (a) (b)
<u>Te</u> taea   <u>Te</u> ueue! (—)

(a)   (b)

Position adopted before 'Pa'

Slap right fist on ground on HEI!

(a)   (b)
<u>I</u> au-<u>e</u>   <u>He</u>i!

Patua i <u>te</u> whenua <u>HEI</u>! (—)

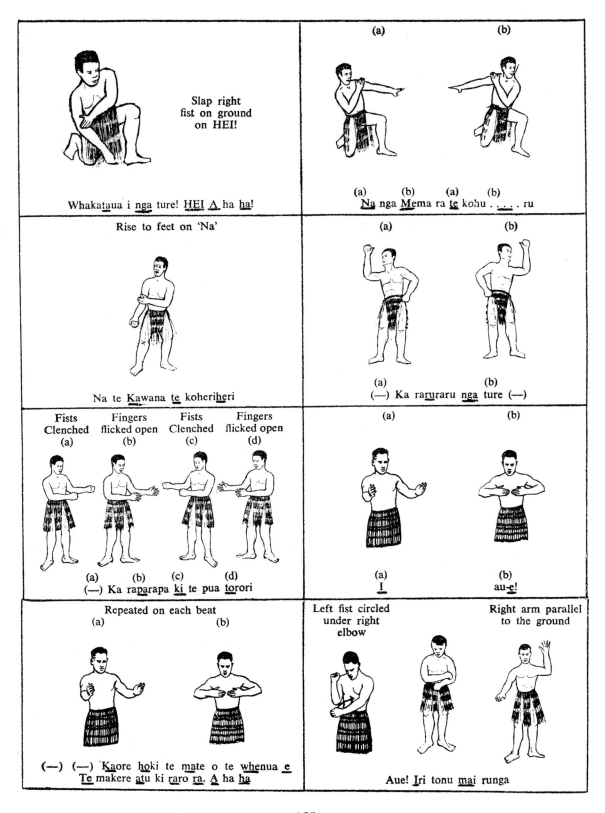

Slap right fist on ground on HEI!

Whaka<u>t</u>aua i <u>nga</u> ture! <u>HEI</u> <u>A</u> ha <u>ha</u>!

(a) (b) (a) (b)
<u>Na</u> nga <u>M</u>ema ra <u>te</u> kohu . . . . . ru

Rise to feet on 'Na'

Na te <u>K</u>awana <u>te</u> koheri<u>h</u>eri

(—) Ka ra<u>ru</u>raru <u>nga</u> ture (—)

Fists Clenched (a)   Fingers flicked open (b)   Fists Clenched (c)   Fingers flicked open (d)

(a) (b) (c) (d)
(—) Ka ra<u>pa</u>rapa <u>ki</u> te pua <u>to</u>rori

(a)   (b)
<u>I</u>   au-<u>e</u>!

Repeated on each beat
(a)   (b)

(—) (—) <u>K</u>aore <u>h</u>oki te <u>m</u>ate o te <u>wh</u>enua <u>e</u>
<u>Te</u> makere <u>a</u>tu ki <u>ra</u>ro <u>ra</u>. <u>A</u> ha <u>ha</u>

Left fist circled under right elbow

Right arm parallel to the ground

Aue! <u>I</u>ri tonu <u>ma</u>i runga

153

(O) te ki<u>ri</u>ngutu <u>mau</u> mai <u>ai</u>

Hei <u>ti</u>pare <u>ta</u>ua ki te <u>ho</u>ariri <u>A</u> ha <u>ha</u>

Right fist
circled under
left elbow

I tahuna <u>mai</u> au

Ki te whakahere <u>to</u>to ko<u>a</u>
<u>E</u> ki te ngakau o <u>te</u> whenua<u>nei</u>
(E) ki te <u>ko</u>ura!

(a)   (b)

(a)   (b) (a) (b)   (a)   (b)
(<u>I</u>) aue, <u>tau</u>kuri e (—) <u>A</u> ha <u>ha</u>!

(a)   (b)

(a)   (b)   (a)   (b)
Ko <u>tu</u>hiki<u>ti</u>a, ko <u>tu</u>hapa<u>i</u>nga,
(a)   (b)   (a)
I <u>ra</u>ro i te w<u>he</u>ro o te Ma . . . . ori!

Right leg gives
a kick. Slap
buttock with right
hand on 'hu'

Huki<u>ti</u>   <u>A</u> ha <u>ha</u>

(a)   (b)

(a)   (b)   (a)   (b)   (a)
<u>Na</u> te ngu<u>tu</u> o te <u>Ma</u>ori <u>po</u>hara, <u>kai</u> kutu
(b)   (a)   (b)   (a)   (b)
(<u>Na</u>) te we<u>ri</u>weri <u>ko</u>' i homa<u>i</u> ke ko<u>nei</u>?

154

(a)   (b)   (a)   (b)
(E) kao<u>re</u> i ara (<u>i</u>) hara<u>mai</u> tonu

(a)   (b)
<u>koe</u> ki te <u>kai</u> when<u>ua</u>!

(a)   (b)   (a)   (b)
(—) Poko<u>ko</u>hua (—) Kaura<u>mo</u>kai

The right fist moves over the top
of the left in a wringing motion

<u>Hei</u>! (—) <u>A</u> ha <u>ha</u>

(a)   (b)
<u>Te</u> puta a<u>tu</u> hoki
(a)   (b)   (a)   (b)   (a)
<u>Te</u> Ihu o te <u>waka</u> i nga (—) toro<u>u</u>ka o N<u>iu</u>
                 (b)
                 Ti<u>re</u>ni

This position is
maintained for the
remainder of the line

(a)   (b)   (c)
Ka <u>pa</u>ia puk<u>u</u>tia (e) nga uau<u>a</u> o te <u>tu</u>re a te
<u>Ka</u>wa<u>na</u>!

(a)   (b)
<u>Te</u> taea   <u>te</u> ueue

(a)   (b)   (c)   (d)
(—) Au   (—) Au   (—) Aue   <u>HEI</u>!

155

22

KUMEKUMEA — A CANOE SONG

According to Sir Apirana Ngata, this haka was first performed with koikoi, or spears, by the East Coast tribes at the reception to the Duke and Duchess of York at Rotorua on 15 June 1901. Since then it has featured at many famous ceremonial occasions, including the welcome to the Queen and the Duke of Edinburgh at Rotorua on 2 January 1954. On this occasion it was performed by the Arawa and Ngati Tuwharetoa tribes. As her majesty advanced across the marae towards the dais, a party of one hundred and forty warriors — the traditional size of the ancient Hokowhitu-a-Tu — performed a bracket of peruperu which consisted of *Kumekumea* and also *Uhi Mai* and *Koia ano* which follow.

The actual words of *Kumekume*, however, date back much further than 1901. It is probably one of the 'to waka' or canoe hauling songs referred to in chapter 18. A free translation is given. The haka may be done as a haka taparahi or as a peruperu. Examples of both are given below.

Kumekumea!	Take the strain!
Totoia!	Draw it thither!
Kumekumea!	Drag it hither!
Totoia!	Haul the canoe from its resting place!
A e to ra	Heave together
Ki te tahataha	To the steep bank which leads to the water
A e to ra	Heave together
Ki te taparere	Over the lip
Nga kokako ki huataratara	Like a shag diving into the ruffled waters of Hua*
Waikurekure ha!	And on to Waikurekure
A ki Waikurekure ha! Hei!	Thence to Waikurekure

*Hua: One of the gods who ruled the tides.

Leader: Kumekumea!
All: Toto-i-a
Repeat
Leader: A e ... to ra
All: Ki te tahataha
Leader: A e ... to ra
All: Ki te taparere
Leader: Nga ... kokako (ki) **Hua** taratara
All: Waikurekure... ha!
                   A ki **Wai**kure**kure ha!**
                   A ki **Wai**kurekure **ha!**

Kaea: Whiti whiti! Kumekumea!

(a)　　　　(b)
Twice
Once for each beat
All: Toto-i-a

(a)　　(b)　　(a)　　(b)
Twice　　　　Twice
Once on each beat　　Once on each beat
Kaea: Kumekumea　　All: Toto-i-a

Kaea: Ae to ra　　All: Ki te tahataha
Kaea: Ae to ra　　All: Ki te taparere

All: Nga. . . .　　kokako　　huataratara

Waikure —　　kure　　Ha!

A. . . . ki　　waikure —　　kure　　Ha!

Hei!

KUMEKUMEA AS A PERUPERU

For the introductory portion shown in these two frames the performers grasp one another's taiaha and work in concert as shown in the sketches. Subsequent actions may be performed individually, that is, with each performer grasping only his own taiaha, or in concert through to the end.

Whiti Whiti	Hei	Ha	Hei

Facing front A gentle pull from left to right	Now lean into it Vigorous hauling action from the left	Facing front A gentle pull from right to left	Now lean into it Vigorous hauling action from the right
Kaea: Kumekumea	**All:** Toto-i-a	**Kaea:** Kumekumea	**All:** Toto-i-a

Facing front A gentle pull from left to right	Now lean into it Vigorous hauling action from the left	Facing front A gentle pull from right to left	Now lean into it Vigorous hauling action from the right
Kaea: Ae to ra	**All:** Ki te tahataha	**Kaea:** Ae to ra	**All:** Ki te taparere

Body upright	Body leaning back
All: Nga. . . . . kokako huataratara	Waikure — kure Ha

A . . . . . . ki   Waikure —   **kure**

Ha!   **He**i!

Kaea: Kei raro!

23

UHI MAI TE WAERO — PERUPERU

As a professional soldier, I have always been filled with admiration at the comparative simplicity of the ancient Maori mobilisation procedures. Tedious formalities were dispensed with and the chief's word was the only proclamation of intention needed. The warriors were always in training, and indeed welcomed the diversion offered by the pursuit of arms. All would gather on the marae, called there by the booming notes of the pahu or war gong, and the chiefs and elders would make fiery speeches interspersed with peruperu and other displays of martial skill.

Kaea:	Whakarongo te taringa	Listen with your ears
Katoa:	Ki te tangi o te huia	To the song of the huia bird
Kaea:	E karanga nei:	'Tis calling now
Katoa:	Huia, huia, huia mai tatou	Let us assemble together
	Tuia, tuia, tuia mai tatou	Let us be bound together in unity
	Tokia, tokia, tokia, HEI!	Let us anoint ourselves!

The last three lines are an ingenious play on the call of the huia, tui and torea birds. At these exhortations to action the warriors will fall in with their chief to proclaim their warlike intentions:

Kaea:	Whiti! Whiti!	Be upstanding
Katoa:	Hei! Ha!	Hei! Ha!
Kaea:	Tenei taku taua	This is my war party
	Uhi, uhi mai te waero e!	Cover me with the dog-skin cloak of battle
Katoa:	E ko roto ko taku puta!	And leap into the fray!
	He puta aha te puta?	The battle, what of it?
	He puta tohu te puta!	Warrior meets warrior!
	E rua nei ko te puta	Man to man
	Ha! Hei!	Ha! The battle is joined!

RHYTHM

U...hi **uhi** mai **te** waero e
E...**ko** roto **ko** taku **puta** (pause)
He puta aha te **pu**ta (pause)
He puta **tohu** te **pu**ta (pause)
E rua **nei** ko te **puta Ha! Hei!**
(from here this peruperu may lead into *Koia Ano*)

160

Whiti! Whiti!

Hei!

Ha!

twice

E
ko taku

ko roto

puta

He puta

aha te

puta

(pause)

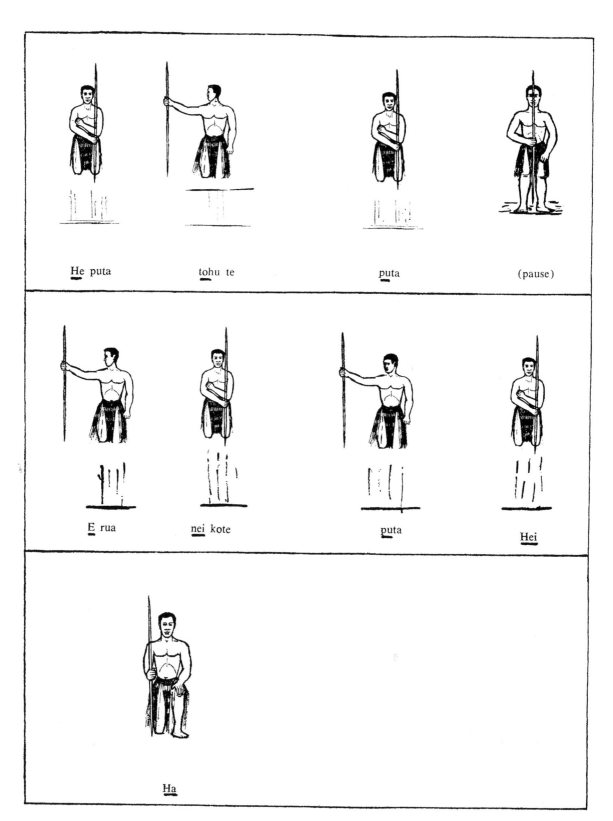

He puta   tohu te   puta   (pause)

E rua   nei kote   puta   Hei

Ha

24

KIA KUTIA — PERUPERU

This is often used as an introduction to longer peruperu. The words are in fact a ngeri or exhortation to the warriors before going into battle. It is of ancient origin. Here is a description by an early writer of a performance he witnessed of this same haka. It vividly captures the atmosphere of the occasion.

'The body of armed men being drawn up in a column, four or five abreast, they remain for some time in a squatting position, which posture corresponds with the stand-at-ease of our soldiers. Suddenly a signal is given by one of the chiefs, who stands in front and shouts out a short sentence in a peculiar measured tone. On the instant he arrives at the last word all start to their legs as one man, and the war song and dance commence. Every right hand brandishes a weapon, whilst the left hands, slapped violently against naked thighs, in the regular time, produce a wild sort of accompaniment to the song. At the words "kia rere" the movement of the actors becomes furious: they leap with fierce gestures, loll their tongues, glare with their eyes ... .'

Kaea:	Whiti whiti HEI!	Stand up and be ready!
	Kia kutia!	Close in
Katoa:	Au! Au!	Yes! Yes!
Kaea:	Kia wherahia!	Fling out (the arms)
Katoa:	Au! Au!	Yes! Yes!
	Kia rere atu te kekeno	Let the seal (i.e. the enemy) fly away
	Ki tawhiti	To the distance
	Titiro mai ai!	And there gaze back (in fear)!
	Ae! Ae! Ae! Ha!	Yes! Yes! Yes!

Rhythm

Kia kutia! **Au! Au!**
Kia whe**ra**hia! **Au! Au!**
Kia rere **a**tu te **ke**keno
Ki tawhiti **ti**tiro **mai ... ai!**
(beat) Ae!
(beat) Ae!
(beat) Aeeee
Ha!

Although this peruperu appears simple, the timing is tricky, as is the coordination of the foot and hand movements. For detail of the foot movement used in this peruperu from 'kia rere' onwards, see page 17.

	All jump to feet Position maintained
Whiti! Whiti!	Hei! Kia kutia!
	 Position maintained
Au!	Au! Kia wherahia
Au!	Au!

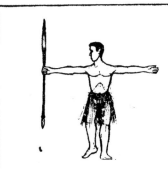

<u>Kia</u>	re -	re
<u>A</u> -	tu	te
<u>Ke</u> -	ke -	no
<u>Ki</u>	ta -	whiti
<u>Ti</u> -	ti -	ro
<u>Ma</u>	i -	i
<u>A</u> -	i -	i
		Ae!
		Ae!
		Ae............

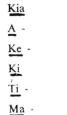

Facing right looking up at taiaha crouching stance. Overhead grip on taiaha.

Face front

eeeeee

Ha

25

KOIA ANO — PERUPERU

Koia Ano is a victory peruperu — a defiant dance of triumph after the successful conclusion of a campaign. It comes from the Ngati Tuwharetoa (Taupo) and Te Arawa (Rotorua) tribal area. Two versions of the peruperu are known to me, although there are others. For ease of reference I have called these two versions A and B.

There is an interesting historical account of a performance of this peruperu. In 1836 an army of Arawa marched against the Ngai Te Rangi tribe and stormed Te Tumu Pa, which stood on a low sandy mound near the beach on the Bay of Plenty coast between Tauranga and Maketu.

This is how Te Araki te Pohu, a chief of the Ngati Tu subtribe of Te Arawa from Owhatiura, near Rotorua, and who had been present at this famous battle, described its aftermath:

'Many of the defenders [of the pa] fled in the direction of Tauranga, but we pursued them along the beach and killed or captured most of them. So fell that fort. They died, they were cooked, they were eaten! After the battle and pursuit we gathered in the conquered pa, the many hundreds of the Arawa, and there we danced our war dance of jubilation and victory. This was the chorus we shouted as we held our weapons horizontally before us with both hands and quickly raised them at arms' length above our heads and down again in time to the song.'

Koia ano!	Yes indeed!
Koia ano!	Yes indeed!
Koia ano he peruperu!	This is our battle dance!
Inahoki ra te taiaroa	Behold my victor weapon
Whakatirohia mai ra	And see this mighty blow,
Ki te whana	And the enemy dead
A ha! Pare-rewha!	That strew our battlefield
Pare-rewha!	
Pare-rewha!	

A song such as this, which exults over victory and upbraids the defeated, is known as 'kotatatara'. It is similar to the 'pioi' sung by successful warriors as they brandished the heads of their slain enemies, and the 'pihe' which was sung over the bodies of the dead.

RHYTHM

	Version A	Version B
Kaea:	Ko – i – a ano	Koia a...no
	Ko – i – a ano	Koia a...no
Katoa:	Ko – a – i – a ano he peruperu	Koai a...no he peruperu (beat)
	Inahoki ra te taia ro a	Inahoki te taia-ro-a... (beat)
	Whakatirohia mai ra	Whaka tirohi-a mai ra
	Ki te whana	Ki te whana
	A ha	A ha
	Pare-rewha	Pare-rewha
	Pare-rewha	Pare-rewha
	Pare-re...wha Hei	Pare-rewha
	Ha	Hei

VERSION A

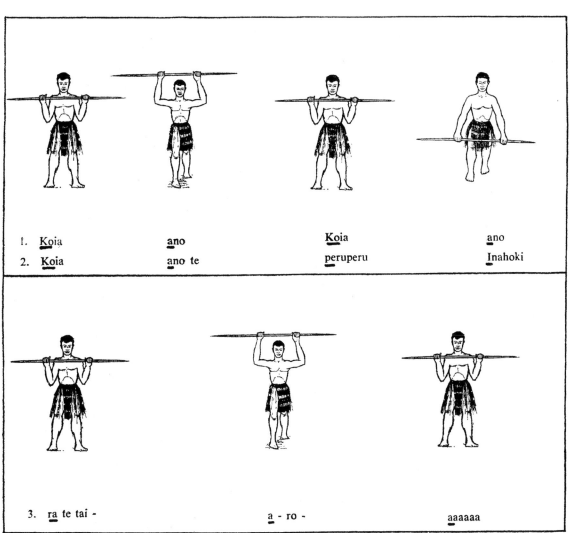

1. Koia   ano   Koia   ano
2. Koia   ano te   peruperu   Inahoki

3. ra te tai -   a - ro -   aaaaaa

From here on, performers leap into the air on each beat and perform actions as below.

4. Whakatiro -   hia mai   na   Ki te whana
5. A ha!   Pare - rewha   Pare - rewha   Pare - reee

Side view
(Performers continue to face front for this action
but for clarity a side view is shown)

wha   Hei!

VERSION B

Kei runga kei raro   Hei!   Ha

168

From here on the weapon is raised and lowered as shown in the two previous sketches, a movement taking place on each beat of the words until . . . . . .

Hei   Ha

The weapon is then thrust out horizontally from the chest to full arms' length on each beat.

Tuwharetoa normally go straight from here into the peruperu "Kume kumea" shown in a previous chapter.

Pare-rewha   Hei

Pare-rewha

Pare-rewha

26

A SELECTION OF WELL-KNOWN HAKA

As has been mentioned elsewhere, the haka taparahi was a dance in which the Maori expressed opinions, emotion, and private and public sentiment of every kind. Those surviving to the present day are but a fraction of the total number which have been composed over the centuries. New taparahi, that is, ones composed over the last fifty years, are practically non-existent. Those that are new are almost entirely adaptations and modernisations of classic taparahi of bygone eras.

Nevertheless, in making the selection for this book there was a very large number from which to choose. Those ultimately selected for illustration are among the best known and most frequently performed. There are many others, however, with just as deserving claims for inclusion which have been excluded because of lack of space. Here, for the purpose of study and comparison, are the words and translation of eight more well known taparahi.

KA PANAPANA

This is a classic women's haka of welcome. This version of the words was the work of Sir Apirana Ngata for the great memorial hui at Whakarua Park, Ruatoria, when the parents of Lieutenant Moana Ngarimu received their son's posthumous Victoria Cross. Note the topical reference to Hitler.

A ra ra! Ka panapana, A ha ha!	Lo, it is throbbing, A ha ha!
Ka rekareka tonu taku ngakau	My heart is throbbing delighted
Ki nga mana ririki i Pohatu-whakapiri	With the common people at Pohatu-whakapiri
Kia haramai te takitini,	Who have come in their multitudes
Kia haramai te takimano,	Who have come in their thousands
Kia paretaitokotia ki Rawhiti!	And alighted upon the Eastern Sea.
Hi! Ha!	Hi Ha!
He mamae, he mamae! A ha ha!	Alas, there is a multitude of pain!
Ka haere, ka haere taku powhiri	My call of welcome goes out
Ki te Tai Whakarunga!	To the Southern Sea!
Hoki mai, hoki mai taku tinana!	But alas comes back to me!
Ka haere, ka haere taku powhiri	My words of welcome go out
Ki te Tai Whakararo!	To the Northern Sea!
Hoki mai, hoki mai taku tinana!	But again come back to me!
Kia huri au ki te tai whakatu a Kupe	So I turn to the sea which Kupe raised up
Ki te tai o Matawhero i motu mai!	To the sea which breaks at Matawhero!
E ko Hitara ki roto ki aku ringa,	There is Hitler within my embrace,
Kutia rawatia kia pari tona ihu!	Where I will crush him and break him!

170

Hi ha! Auhi ana! Kss! Kss! Hei!
Kia whakanga hoki au i ahau
I aue! Hei!

Hi Ha! It is fitting!
Now let me pause and rest awhile
Down, down, down to the ground.

HAUKIWI HAUWEKA

This is another haka powhiri or women's haka of welcome. It is an adaptation of an ancient haka.
Sir Apirana Ngata called it 'the very a b c of posture dancing, devised by the wise men of old to
exemplify rhythm of movement and the suiting of action to words and words to action.'

Haukiwi, hauweka, kawea he korero
Kia whakaronga mai—
Nga iwi o te motu, pakia!
Aue! E te tai whakarunga!
E te tai whakararo!
Ka pupuru tonu.
Te huka tai moana nui aue!
Nga iwi whakakeke o Aotearoa
Huri ke, anga ke!
He paruparu no te Tai Rawhiti
Kia ruku mai koe!
Ana to kai! Ana to kai! Aue hei!

Softly blowing winds take these words
So that the scattered tribes may hear,
People of this land, strike your thighs!
People of the southern sea!
People of the northern tide!
The waves are breaking along the shores,
Hearken, ye stubborn tribes of New Zealand
Who turn this way and that!
Risking it may be a fall!
Here is the mud of the Eastern Sea
Through which you may plunge!
There is your food! There is your food!

KURA TIWAKA TAUA

This is one of a great trilogy of classic taparahi, the others being *Ruaumoko* and *Te Kiringutu*. From
the line 'He tia, he tia, he tia' the haka is actually the ancient tupa waka, or canoe-hauling chant,
which according to legend was used to launch the *Takitimu* canoe in far-off Hawaiki, legendary
homeland of the Maori. Much of the haka is archaic and difficult to translate. This is another
Ngata adaptation from the Ngarimu hui, and the young Victoria Cross winner is symbolised
as the kai kakariki, or canoe leader, commanding and inspiring the crews of five of the canoes
during the heke or Great Migration of the fourteenth century. The translation is Ngata's.

Whakaara
Ma konei ake au!
Titaha ake ai, hai!
Me kore e tutaki!
He pupu karikawa,
He pupu harerorero hai!
Ka tikoki! Ka tahuri!
Ka tahuri ra Niu Tireni, i aue!

The Rising
Let me proceed by this way!
Sidling along!
Perhaps I shall meet there
Some ancient,
Lolling his tongue at me!
It is heeling over! It has capsized!
New Zealand has capsized over! Aue!

171

Taparahi

Papa te whatitiri, hikohiko te uira
I kanapu ki te rangi,
I whetuki raro ra,
Ru ana te whenua, e!
E, i aha tera e! Ko te werohanga
A Porourangi i te Ika a Maui
E takoto nei! A ha ha!
Kia anga tiraha ra to puku ki runga ra!
A ha ha! Kia eke mai o iwi ki runga
Ki to tuatua werowero ai e ha!
I aue, taukuri, e!
Tena ra, e tama! Tu ake ki runga ra
Ki te hautu i ohou waka, i a Horouta,
Takitimu, Mataatua, Tainui, Te Arawa,
E takoto nei! A ha ha!
Aue! He tia, he tia, he tia!
Aue! He ranga, he ranga, he ranga!
Whakarere iho ana te kakau o te hoe
Ko maninitua! Ko maniniaro!
Tangi te kura i tangi wiwini,
Tangi te kura i tangi wawana!
Tera te haeata takiri ana mai
I runga o Hikurangi!
Aha! Whaiuru, whaiuru, whaiuru!
Aha Whaiato, whaiato, whaiato!
Arara tini! Arara tini! Ara ri!
A ko tena, tena! A ko tena, tena!
Ehara ko te wai o to waha,
Ko te wai o to waha!
Hei koti, hei koti, hei koti!
Ka rere! I ka rere!
Te rere i te waka, kutangitangi!
E kura tiwaka taua! (twice)
E kura wawawa wai! (twice)

The Body of the Taparahi

The thunder crashes, the lightning flashes
Illuminating the heavens,
While the shock strikes earth
Which trembles and quakes, ha!
So nature bears witness that Porourangi
Has pierced the great Fish of Maui
Which lies beneath us! A ha ha!
So 'tis your belly upturned and laid bare
So that your people may mount
And spear you!
A ha ha!
Arise then my son and take your stand
To direct and urge on your canoes, Horouta,
Takitimu, Mataatua, Tainui, Te Arawa,
The great fleet drawn up here!
Striking, sweeping, paddling!
Down dips the blade of the paddle
Sweeping behind, flashing before!
The speeding canoe sings in the wind,
Vibrant, it chants to the breeze
Behold the first light of dawn
Is reflected from the crest of Hikurangi!
A ha ha! Dipping close to this side!
Now changing and plunging to that side!
Urging and urging the canoe on!
Now faster and faster!
It is not like the foam from your mouth,
Thrown out, expelled with force!
So it speeds, so it speeds—
So my canoe rushes swiftly on!
For it is the canoe of war!
It is the master of the seas!
Cleaving the ocean waves,
Parting the wild rushing seas!

KO TE IWI MAORI

This is a very simple haka often performed as an introduction to other more complex taparahi.

Ko te iwi Maori e ngunguru nei!	It is the Maori people growling here
Au! Au! Aue ha!	Au! Au! Aue ha!
Ko te iwi Maori e ngunguru nei!	It is the Maori people gnashing their teeth
Au! Au! Aue ha!	Au! Au! Aue ha!
A ha ha!	A ha ha!
Ka tu te ihihi,	The sun scatters its rays,
Ka tu te wanawana,	The many-coloured rainbow appears,
Ki runga ki te rangi,	In the deep vault
E tu iho nei, i aue!	Of the heavens above.

HUA ATU AU KO MATARIKI

This is another example of an ancient haka taparahi, with words adapted to include a contemporary enemy of the Maori people.

Hua atu au ko Matariki, ko Autahi	Methought 'twas Pleiades or Canopus, twas
Ko te whetu haere i te taha o te rangi	The star that roams the wide horizon;
Ka tineia mai e te ahi a Mahuika,	The star that was dimmed by Mahuika's flames!
Pakia!	But lo! 'Tis a taniwha appears, 'tis
Whakakau he taniwha, hei!	Yea, a dragon approaching!
Whakakau he taniwha, hei!	'Tis the famed war party of Tu
Whakakau ko te Hokowhitu a Tu	Which draws nigh to land at Poneke.
Ka u to tira kei Poneke.	Clap your hands!
Pakia!	You have scaled the very heights
Piki mai, kake mai i nga	Of far-off Italy.
Pikitanga kei Itari.	And descended to Germany's plains.
Whakaheke tonu to haere ki Tiamana.	A ha ha! Bring with you
A ha ha! A mauria mai ra	The power of Hitler
Te mano o Hitara	The cause of this bitter strife.
Nana nei ko te pakanga ka tu.	Hi aue!
Hi aue!	Hither now come the warriors,
Haere mai ana nga toa,	Borne on the wings of the winds,
I runga i te upoko hau,	Borne on the wave of the tempest,
I te pa marangai,	Borne by the power of love.
I te puehutanga mai o te aroha,	They assemble at Rotorua,
Ka u whakarauri ki Rotorua,	The guests are filling the house
Ka ki te whare i te manuhiri,	Let your eyes be filled
Uhia mai, uhia mai o kanohi	With good fellowship;
Ki te rau o te aroha;	For the scales of Maui's fish
Ki te unahi o te Ika-a-Maui Tikitiki	Visible before us!
E tu ake nei!	For the mortal and the immortal
He atua, he tangata, he atua, he tangata	Hi aue!
Hi aue!	

HE MANGUMANGU TAIPO

This haka taparahi belongs to the people of Taranaki and Whanganui area, who claim descent from their ancestral canoe *Aotea*. It is an injunction against too close an identification with Pakeha ways of life.

Whakarongo mai te iwi nei	Hearken to me, ye tribes,
Whakarongo mai te motu nei	Hear my voice, ye of this land,
Ahakoa whakapiri koe ki a tauiwi;	Though you associate yourself with strangers,
E kore e taka te ingoa Maori i runga i a koe.	You will not lose the name 'Maori'
He mangumangu taipo nei hoki tatou pakia	For we are dark skinned fellows, no less*
Te kupu a Tohu ki nga iwi e rua;	Tohu† had this to say of the two races:
'E kore e piri te uku ki te rino,	'Clay cannot adhere iron to iron,
Ka whitingia e te ra, ka ngahoro.'	For as soon as the sun shines on it, it will fall.'

TE TANGI MAI

This is a kaioraora, or taparahi of defiance or abuse, and may be compared with *Te Kiringutu*. It was recorded by Elsdon Best, who lived for many years among the Tuhoe Maori of the Urewera. He tells that when the first Land Commission visited that tribe a considerable stir was created and many old feuds were revived which gave rise to several haka similar to this. When the commissioners were ceremonially received by the tribe, a long procession of young men, barelegged and naked to the waist, came onto the marae and performed this haka.

Te tangi mai a te ika nei a te poraka	We are croaking as does the frog
A, ku-ke-ke…e!	Croak croak!
Ku-keke-keke a Tuhoe ki Te Whaiti,	Tuhoe are croaking at Te Whaiti
A, ku-ke-ke…e!	Croak croak!
Titiro ki runga! Titiro ki raro!	Look up and look down!
Titiro ki te mana motuhake e rere mai nei e!	Gaze at the special power flying yonder!
Hihi ana mai te pene a te Komihana …	Listen to the pen of the Commissioner
A, hihi ana mai! Aue!	As it goes 'hihi' scratch, scratch.

In the initial part of the haka, Tuhoe compare themselves to frogs, which, according to Best, were rapidly multiplying in the district at that time. The Te Whaiti referred to was a block of land claimed by three hapu, or family groups, and the cause of a great deal of ill feeling. The 'special power' was a flag on which were inscribed the words, 'Te Mana motuhake mo Tuhoe'— the special prestige belonging to Tuhoe. This flag had been presented to the tribe by the Government. 'Hihi' is onomatopoeic, a sound word improvised to evoke the scratching made by a quickly writing pen.

These notes show why it is often so difficult to translate haka without knowledge of their origins and the significance of their composition.

* Meaning nothing can alter the colour of Maori skin.
† Tohu was a local prophet of Taranaki.

KO RANGINUI TE ATUA or WAKA ATUA

This is the adaptation of this taparahi which was used for two Royal visits. Hence the reference to the Queen symbolised as the White Heron of single flight. In a slightly shortened form a Ngati Akarana Party from Auckland performed it at Waitangi on 6 February 1963 before the Queen, and the version below was featured by the Taihauauru tribes from the West Coast of the North Island at the great Rotorua Royal Hui on 2 January 1954. It was specially composed for this latter occasion by Arapeta Awatere, probably the foremost modern composer of Maori music and haka.

Ko Ranginui te Atua	Ranginui is the God
Ko Papatuanuku te wahine	Papatuanuku is the Goddess
A ha ha! Ka tuku taku ihi atua	They reared my divine ancestors
Ka tuku taku ihi he tangata	They reared my human ancestors,
Ki te Whaiao	Into this world of form
Ki te Ao Marama	Into this world of light
He atua, he tangata, ho!	Some where of the Gods and some were of men.
Ko Tangaroa, ko Haumiatiketike	There is Tangaroa, also Haumiatiketike,
Ko Ruaumoko e hu nei taku potiki, hu!	Then Ruamoko roaring there, our lastborn!
Tanemahuta, Tawhirimatea,	Tanemahuta, Tawhirimatea.
Ko Tumatauenga	There is Tumatauenga (God of War)
Ngangahu ake nei te weriweri	He pouts this ugly one,
Ngangahu ake nei te tipua	He grimaces this ruthless one,
Ka tu te ihiihi, ka tu te wanawana,	Spreading fear and terror afar,
Ki runga ki te rangi e tu iho nei! Hei!	Even unto the sky which stretches above!
Whakakau aku waka, hei!	My canoes have travelled
Takitimu, Te Arawa, Tainui, Mataatua,	The names which I list here:
Horouta, Kurahaupo, Tokomaru, Aotea	Takitimu, Te Arawa, Tainui, Mataatua,
Ka u aku waka ki te Pono-o-Tamatekapua	Horouta, Kurahaupo, Tokomaru, Aotea.
Tuwhera kau ake ra!	Now they have beached in the realm of
Kumekumea, totoia! I au e, hei!	Tamatekapua, so hospitable there.
Ko wai tera whakarewarewa maiangi,	Haul them ashore, drag them ashore.
Kokiri ake te haeata, ka mahuta mai te pae?	Who art thou that cometh soaring,
Ko taku kotuku rerenga tahi!	Heralding the dawn from yon horizon?
Haramai koe i tawhiti nui,	'Tis the white heron of single flight,
Haramai koe i tawhiti roa,	You have come a long way,
Piki mai ra, kake mai ra	Come to us, be with us!
Piki ake kake ake, i au e, hei!	Come with us, be with us!
Haramai te manuhiri turau taimano	Come thou guest illustrious, serene,
Rarunga mai, te Tiriti o Waitangi, a ha ha!	Nigh o'er the Treaty of Waitangi,
Ko te taoroa tena a to tipuna a Wikitoria,	That was the spear of thine ancestress, Victoria.
Tukitukia, werowerohia ake te Ika-a-Maui,	Smitten, pierced by it was Maui's fish
Tiraha kau ake ra!	Thus lying there!
Piki mai ra, kake mai ra, piki ake, kake ake i au e!	Come unto us, welcome welcome!
No Tuawhakarere to ihi, to wehi, to mana!	Age-old are thy prestige, reverence, sovereignty.

Haramai tonu kia kite koe i aku ngarara,
No Tuainuku, he taniwha! He mokomoko! He tuatara!
Kai, hau, kai po,
Rere ana te wehiwehi! I au e, hei!
Kanga mai nga iwi katoa ki …
Taku upoko.
He tapu nei hoki …
Taku upoko.
No tuainuku …
Taku upoko.
No tuairangi …
Taku upoko.
A ha ha! E kai o niho ki te whetu,
E kai o niho ki te marama,
Piki tonu, heke tonu ki te Reinga.

Welcome, thou shalt meet my reptiles,
From remote ages they descend!
They devour the wind, yea and darkness also
Awe-inspiring, yes indeed!
All the tribes are cursing …
My head.
Sacred is …
My head.
From ages remote is …
My head.
From ages unknowable is …
My head.
See there, let your teeth sink into the star,
Let your teeth sink into the moon,
Rise up, descend to the nether world!

GLOSSARY

This glossary contains a selection of Maori words pertaining to Maori games, songs and dances. Many of the words are contained in the text, with or without explanation. Others are synonymous with the words in the text but have not been mentioned there to avoid confusion. Many of the terms for the various Maori dances are used loosely and with varying connotations between tribes. An attempt has been made wherever possible to define and differentiate between these terms. Some of the definitions, however, will be open to discussion.

Apakura, n. Lament
  Te Tangi a Apakura. The wailing of Apakura (a person in mythology), which denotes the moaning of the seas, a sound associated with sadness and death.
Araara, n. Rising of a body of men for the war dance. See beginning of *Ruaumoko* and *Te Kiringutu.*
Aroarowhaki, v.i. To move the hands with a quivering motion as in haka.

Hahani, n. Song for the purpose of shaming a person for a wrong committed.
Hai, n. The name of the principal stone in the game of ruru.
Haka, v.i. Dance; to sing a song to be accompanied by dance. n. Dance; song accompanying a dance.
  haka aroaroakapa. Posture dance with performers in two ranks.
  haka koiri. A haka containing swaying motions.
  haka horuhoru. A haka in which performers kneel.
  haka matohi. A haka performed by men only in which they stoop and elevate their posteriors in an absurd manner.
  haka pikari. A haka which includes leg movements not seen in other haka.
  haka pirori. A haka accompanied by an incisive virulent song to avenge some insult.
  haka poi. Dance in which the poi ball is used (see chapter 11).
  haka porowha. Haka in which the performers form a square facing four ways
  haka taparahi. Shouted posture dance, without weapons, generally performed today (see part 4).
  haka tutohu. A haka performed as a divinatory exercise by persons grouped in wedge formation.
  haka waiata. A dance accompanied by a mild rhythmical song. It was the forerunner of the modern action song (see chapter 12).
Hakiparepare, n. A hand game (see chapter 6).
Hakirara or hakurara, n. A light song.
Harakoa, n. Dancing and other amusements.
Hari, v.i. To dance, sing a song to dance to. n. Dance; song sung on joyful occasions.
Hari-kai, n. Food-bearing chant.
Hautu (waka), n. A song to give the time to rowers of a canoe.
Hei Tama Tu Tama, n. A hand game (see chapter 6).
Hi, v.t. To lead a song.
Hianga, n. The meaningless particles frequently inserted in a Maori song.
Hikitorea, n. Dirge accompanied with extravagant getures.
Himene, n, Hymn.
Hipitoitoi, n. A hand game (see chapter 6).
Hongi, v.t. and n. Salute by pressing (not rubbing) the nose against that of another.

Hope, n. Waist; loins.

Huhu or huhi, n. Another name for whai or string game.

Huripapa, n. The name for the first movement in the Ngati Porou version of knucklebones. Sometimes used for whole game.

Kaea, n. The leader of a flock of parrots. Hence, used to denote the fugleman or leader in a haka or action song.

Kai-kakariki, n. The man who called the time during the paddling of a canoe. Nowadays sometimes used for the leader of a haka or action song.

Kai-makamaka. A name for the East Coast version of knucklebones (see chapter 5).

Kaioraora, n. A cursing song or song of defiance.

Kaipara, n. Athletic games.

Kaitaki; kaitataki, n. A haka, etc., leader.

Kakapa, n. The vibrating movement of the hands during an action song or a haka.

Kani, kanikani, v.t. To dance.

Kaparoa, n. A movement in the game of knucklebones.

Karakia, n. Charm, spell, incantation, also a ritualistic chant, v.i. Repeat a form of words as chant or spell. v.t. Repeat an incantation over a person.

Karanga, v.t. To call; to welcome. Used in this book to denote the call of welcome which is an integral part of the welcome ceremony.

Katoa. Everyone; all together.

Kaupapa, n. The original of a song as opposed to a parody or later adaptation.

Keka, n. Dirge or lament.

Kohau, v.i. To sing aimlessly, as when travelling alone.

Koikoi, n. A long spear (see chapter 15). Often used in peruperu.

Koki, v.i. To sing in the early morning.

Koko, v.i. To chant for the purpose of keeping the guard awake in wartime.

Ko Kumara, n. Chant by those preparing ground for the kumara crop.

Komekome, n. A game played by opening and shutting the fingers.

Konewa, n. The habit of singing while near the house out of doors. It was regarded as a bad omen.

Kori, Korikori, v.i. To move, wriggle; use action in oratory. The term waiata kori is the generally accepted Maori term for an action song in the modern sense.

Korowhiti, korohiti, v.i. To spring up suddenly from a crouching position, such as in certain haka taparahi, e.g., *Ruaumoko*.

Koruru, n. The term for the Ngai Tahu version of knucklebones (see chapter 5).

Kotaratara, n. A taparahi of triumph such as *Ka Mate* (see chapter 19).

Kotiritiri, n. A game played with light sticks weighted at one end and which are made to bob up and down in a pool of water.

Ku, n. A hand game; also reputed to be a one-string instrument played by tapping with a stick. v.i. To play at ku which was similar to ti ringaringa.

Kurawiniwini, n. A children's game.

Kurupakara, n. A game.

Maimai, n. A taparahi to welcome guests at a tangi.

Maimai aroha, n. A song which is a token of affection.

Maire, n. A song.

Makamaka Whana, v.i. To dance the war dance.

Manatunga, n. Expression of resentment in song or dance performed to keep such resentment alive.

Manawa Wera, n. A song deriding members of a defeated war party and sung by relatives of those who did not return. The singers dressed in old, dirty clothes for the occasion.

Maori. Originally meant ordinary or normal (hence he tangata Maori, an ordinary man, not a foreigner); now refers in normal usage to the indigenous inhabitants of New Zealand and the Cook Islands. Word is pre-European and first applied to themselves by the Maori after the coming of the European. This usage dates from about 1850.

Maoritanga. The condition of being a Maori; Maoriness; Maoridom; all that which makes a Maori a Maori rather than a Pakeha. Maori culture generally.

Marae, n. Lit. the courtyard in front of the meeting house. The Maori equivalent of the 'village square'. Nowadays used for any place where Maori ceremonial is enacted or Maori people meet together.

Te kawa o te marae: marae etiquette.

Mata; matakite, n. A prophetic song.

Mataara, Whakaaraara. Song of a watchman.

Matemate, matimati, n. A hand game (see chapter 6).

Mate rawa. A hand game.

Matohi, n. A dance performed only by men who elevated and lowered their posteriors in a peculiar manner called whakaene.

Maui, n. Another name for Maori string games.

Mere, n. A type of Maori club (see chapter 15).

Moteatea, n. A lament.

Moteko, whakamoteko, v.i. Make grimaces as in haka.

Motiha, n. A dance.

Mu Torere, n. A Maori game (see chapter 5).

Neke, v.i. and v.t. To move. Often called out as a command to move a group on or off a stage during the course of a performance.

Neneke, v.i. To vibrate, as of the hands during a haka, etc.

Ngahau, n. Dance.

Whakangahau, v.i. To amuse, lead by example as in haka, etc.

Ngangahu, v.i. To distort the features as in a haka.

Ngaoraora. As for ngangahu.

Ngaoriori, n. Nursing song, lullaby.

Ngarahu, ngarehu, n. Leader or commander as in a haka (not a common usage). Also Kaingarahu, n. war dance with the generally accepted specialised meaning of a dance with weapons which was by way of an inspection of the war party. Also tutu ngarahu, ngarahu taua.

Ngari, n. Song.

Ngari Tititouretua. Song accompanying a certain type of stick game.

Ngaringari, n. Song to make people pull together.

Ngeri, n. A rhythmic chant with actions with the generally accepted specialised meaning of a song with exhorts, thus:

Ngeri taua, n. Song to exhort a war party before battle.

Ngeri to, n. Song for launching a canoe (urging those hauling it to the water).

Onioni, v.i. Movement and wriggling of a lascivious type used in some haka (the word also means to copulate).

Oriori. v.t. To chant a lullaby. n. Chant, song (not confined, but generally applied to a lullaby).

Oriori potaka, n. Song used while spinning tops.

Whakaoriori, n. Chant or song used for a wide range of purposes.

Pa, n. A Maori fortified village of olden times.

Pahu, n. A war alarm in the form of a wood or stone gong.

Pakeha, n. a. A word derived possibly from pakehakeha meaning a man-like imaginary being with a fair skin. A non-Maori New Zealander.

Pakipaki, v.t. Slap, tap or pat frequently. Many haka and games begin with pakipaki of hands against the thigh.

Pana, n. Repellent song.

Pao, v.t. Sing n: A derisive song and dance.

Papaki, n. A game played by two players clapping the hands in unison.

Para, n. A game in which darts were thrown from one person tol another, v.i. Practise the use of weapons.

Parawhakawai, n. Trials of skill in games.

Patere, n. An abusive song; a dance with grotesque gestures.

Patokotoko, panokonoko, n. A simple string game played by two persons.

179

Patu, n. Short club (see chapter 15). Often carried by haka leaders.

Pekerangi, n. and v.t. A dance accompanied by a song; to perform such a dance.

Perepere, n. The counters or 'men' used in the game of mu torere.

Peruperu, n. The shouted war dance with weapons.

Pihe, n. A lament sung over the bodies of those killed in battle and accompanied by the waving of arms to denote grief.

Pikari, vi. Grimacing during the haka by rolling the eyes. n. The grimace by rolling the eyes.

Pioi, n. A song sung while brandishing head or scalp of enemy.

Pioriori, n, A song perhaps sung over the bodies of those killed in battle.

Piripiri, n. A game resembling hide and seek.

Piro, a. Out, in games, n. Victory in games.

Pitau, pitautau, n. Snatch of a song.

Piu, v.i. Skipping, Maori fashion.

Piupiu, n. The modern dance costume, consisting of the dried and rolled leaves of the flax bush attached to a waistband. It reaches to just above the knees for men and to mid-calf length for women. About four hundred leaves may go into a good piupiu. Portions of the leaves are scraped and dried, and dyed black to form a pattern on the garment.

Popo, n. A lullaby.

Pohane, n. Love song.

Pohi, n. A type of song.

Poi, n. A small ball made of fabric and used in the haka poi (see chapter 11).

Pongara, n. Game.

Poteketeke; Poteketeke, n. An indecent dance in which the naked performers executed grotesque movements; also a performer out in front of a haka leading the rest.

Powhiri, pohiri, n. A dance or song, welcome, the whole ceremony of welcome. v.t. To welcome, to beckon anyone to come on.

Puha, n. Song, chant, sometimes accompanied by a war dance.

Pukana, v.i. To distort the features as in a haka. In a narrower sense it means grimacing by rolling and protruding the eye-balls; also to make contortions of the face as an amusement.

Punipuni, n. A game played by two players seated opposite and facing one another. Each holds up a hand with fingers out stretched. One holds his hand steady while the other, with eyes closed, attempts to pass the fingers of his hand between those of his opponent's hand.

Rangi, n. Air, tune, stanza, division or portion of a song.

Rangi Koauau, n. Song accompanying flute playing.

Rangi Pakuru, n. Song accompanied by tapping on two sticks, one of which is held between the teeth and tapped with the other.

Rangi Poi, n. Poi song.

Rangirangi, n. A song to enable paddlers to keep time.

Rehia, n. Pleasure, amusement, enjoyment, play.
Nga mahi a te rehia. The pursuit of pleasure.
Whare rehia, n. A building set aside for games and dances.

Rehu, v.t. To sing; chant.

Ropu, n. A choir.

Ruri, ruriruri, n. Song, ditty, generally a love ditty, sometimes accompanied by arm actions.

Ruru, n. A game similar to knucklebones (see chapter 5).

Tahu, v.i. Make grimaces in a dance.

Taiaha, n. Long club (see chapter 15).

Taiapo, n Lullaby.

Takahi, v.i. Dance; lit. stamp.

Taki, n. The challenge when a visitor moves onto a marae.

Taki manawa, n. Childish amusement of attempting a long jingle in one breath.

Takitaki, v.t. Recite a song.

Tama Tu Tama, n. Hand game (see chapter 6).

Tangi, lit. v.i. To cry; n. Maori funeral ceremony. n. All laments and dirges. A generic term.

tangi maru. A type of lament with wailing.

tangi taukuri. Song expressing self-pity.

tangi tikapa: Tangi Whakakurepe, n. A wordless wailing accompanied by swaying of the body and hand quivering.

tangi whakahoro. Similar to tangi maru.

Tau, v.t. Sing; sing of. n. Ceremonial song.

tau marae. Song introduced into a formal speech of welcome to visitors or introduced during a speech concerned with marae ceremonial.

tau manu. Semi-sacred chant used by bird catchers on returning from the bush and before re-entering their village.

tau (or to) waka. Song to keep time when hauling a canoe.

Tauparoro, n. A game in which one player, by moving his hand quickly, tries to avoid downward strokes with a stick.

Tautapa, v.i. Chant a song for the purpose of keeping tempo in any group activity.

Tautitotito, v.t. Sing songs in response to one another; recite alternately verses or parts of a song. n. A song so sung. Called also waiata tautitotito.

Tewha, n. Any working song but particularly for agricultural work.

Tewhatewha, n. Long club (see chapter 15).

Ti, n. Games sometimes called ti takaro.

Tira, n. Choir.

Ti rakau, n. A general term for stick games, sometimes used for a specific game.

Ti ringaringa, n. Game played by opening and shutting the hands in time to recited verses.

Titi, n. Sticks used in ti rakau.

Tititai, n. Canoe song.

Titi torea, n. A stick game.

To, n. Any hauling song.

Toiere, v.i. Sing, particularly hautu. n. Song for encouraging and giving time to paddlers.

Tokere, n. Pieces of wood or bone, a pair in each hand, used as castanets; a game played by drawing a leaf through the closed fist and guessing at which point the end of the leaf is reached.

Tukeka, n. Lament, dirge.

Tuki waka, n. Song for giving time to paddlers.

Tuki, v.t. Give time to paddlers by song and gesture.

Tumoto, n. Virulent song chanted as revenge for some injury or defeat.

Tupa, tipa, n. Chant, song.

Tupa waka. Song for launching a canoe.

Tupaoe, n. Voices heard singing at night, either supernatural or of persons travelling. v.i. Sing while travelling at night.

Tupeke, n. War dance.

Tuporo, v.i. Sing while travelling.

Turanga-a-Tohu, Tutohu, n. Divinatory dance.

Tutara, n. Song composed by a deserted or wronged husband and directed against his wife.

Tutu, n. Move with vigour.

Tutu waewae, v.i. Dance or war dance. n. Steps of the war dance.

Tutu ngarahu, Ngarehu (see Ngarahu).

Tutukai, n. Guessing game. Stones are passed around a circle of players from hand to hand. When jingle ceases, one player has to guess who holds the stone.

Umanga, n. Song praying for destruction of the enemy.

Umere, v.i. Sing or chant; to keep time in any group effort. n. Song expressing pleasure at a good haul of fish.

Waiata, n. Song. This is by far the most commonly used term. v.t., v.i. To sing.

waiata aroha, n. Love song.

waiata karakia. Charm.

waiata mate kanehe. Song expressing affectionate longings.

waiata popo. Lullaby.

waiata tangi. Lament.

waiata whaiaipo. Love song.

waiata whaiwhaia. A chant in connection with black magic.

waiata whakamanawa taonga. Song sung when accepting a formal gift.

Wero, n. Challenge as visitors enter the marae.

Weru, n. Grimaces during haka caused by pouting and projecting the lips.

Whai, n. General term for Maori string games.

Whaikorero, n. Formal speeches or speech-making.

Whakaaraara (pa); Mataara pa, n. Chant to keep the watch awake or give alarm in war time.

Whakaene, v.i. To present the posteriors in derision as in haka pirori.

Whakahauhau, n. Set song for inspiring workers.

Whakamenemene, v.i. Make grimaces as in haka.

Whakarewarewa, n. War dance to make a show of force before attacking.

Whakatakiri, n. Song sung to a child while it is being dandled.

Whakatapatapa Kumara, n. Song in connection with the planting of kumara.

Whakatea, n. A song of derision sung to returning members of a defeated war party.

Whakaupoko, n. Division or verse of a song.

Whakawai, n. Song sung to comfort a person being tattooed. Also called 'whakawai tanga moko'.

Wiri, wiriwiri, n. The vibrating movement of the hands during haka or action song. This is the most common term of many for this.